NOR ANY OTHER CREATURE

A NOVEL OF SCIENTIFIC IMAGINATION AND CHRISTIAN POSSIBILITY

EARL LEONARD LANGGUTH

Zeta Publishing

Ocala, FL

Zeta Publishing, Inc
3850 SE 58th Ave
Ocala, FL 34480
www.zetapublishing.com

This is a work of fiction. All of the characters, names, incidents, organizations, and dialogue in this novel are either the products of the author's imagination or are used fictitiously.

Ordering Information:
Quantity sales. Special discounts are available on quantity purchases by corporations, associations, and others. For details, contact the publisher at the address above.
Orders by U.S. trade bookstores and wholesalers. Please contact
Zeta Publishing: Tel: (352) 694-2553; Fax: (352) 694-1791 or visit
www.zetapublishing.com

ISBN: 978-1-7335084-4-5 (sc)

ISBN: 978-1-7335084-5-2 (e)

Library of Congress Control Number: 2018968364

Printed in the United States of America

"Amnesia" was what I thought to dread,

That mind should cease to call up memory;

"Omnesia" is mine, and so much worse–

For all the world has now forgotten me.

(*Found scrawled on a motel notepad in Denver after the*

church-sponsored indigent had checked out.)

PROLOGUE

Lewis stepped onto the railroad tracks and began to stride over the uneven ties. He was still anxious and upset. The gleaming moonlit rails propelled him forward, as if he were late. Yet he knew he was right on schedule. Gary already waited for him at his cousin's house, and tomorrow would be the first day of the future entirely his own.

Those last heated words with his father filled his mind with renewed anger, as they had been doing all day. Who would find his note? Probably Mom, and he could imagine what Dad would say when he found out that his oldest son had gone off to join the Navy. Still, his father should not be surprised, after the row they had had at the store. Now his Dad would have to accept that he was a man. He had finished high school and deserved to be treated as an adult!

His fingers were cramping, so he switched the suitcase to his other hand as he hurried along the ties. Ahead stretched the gravel pathway between the steel rails, opening to his future.

Tomorrow he and Gary would enlist. The next time he came home it would be as a sailor who had made a place for himself in the world. Let Dad find out how much he needed his son in the Feed Store, now that he had to do without him!

He peered ahead in the darkness. No train would be coming along tonight, but if one should, he would have plenty of time to jump out of the way. He was glad he had worn his heaviest coat. Not that he would need it, where he was going. Uncle Sam would see to all his clothing needs for the next several years. Those peacoats sailors wore were really great.

Who could tell when he might come home again? Maybe by then

he would have found a girl to marry. Maybe even they would have a baby to bring with them. Mom would enjoy having her first grandchild. Maybe this would soften Dad, and make coming home easier.

There ahead loomed the old tree nearest the right of way that marked the half way point. Soon he would be with Gary, and their adventure would really begin.

At that moment, without the slightest warning, the upper branches of the old tree exploded like a nuclear blast—a world-ending holocaust of sound, light, impossible heat, and shattering force. Lewis never saw it, for he was gone.

Gone, as if he had never been.

The flash died quickly, but the immense noise continued to echo from the distant hills. It also finally faded to a shocked silence.

Moments later, in the distance, a dog began to howl.

ONE

◆

John did not know it yet, but he had just been born.

This life began for John with a dawning awareness of light and consciousness of sound. Unlike others just newly born, he already knew that if he opened his eyes he could see, and he expected to recognize what he was seeing. He knew already where the sounds were coming from. He identified the distant brassy protest of a car unexpectedly denied its rightful place in the stream of merging, moving traffic. He distinguished the starting roar of a diesel truck near at hand. He heard the high social chirping of a flock of birds that had exchanged the clean trees God originally made for them for polluted urban opportunities. These soloists stood out against the unfigured bass of the other noises of a city downtown.

John thought his first thought: "This is what I expect in a city, this time of the morning"

Morning. There was brightness, but it was still edged with the chill of the night just ended. Welcome warmth crept over him; he would open his eyes upon clear skies and sunshine.

In a city.

What city? He did not know where he was, or how he came to be there. He did not yet know himself to be newly born. He turned from questioning to feeling, and sank back into the pleasant sensations of being. Wherever he was, he was here. The concrete under his legs was still chilly; the wall his shoulders were leaning against, rough with decaying stucco. He flexed his leg and it rustled under newspapers he must have covered himself with for warmth during the night. He had endured. Another day had come. Painfully squinting against the glare he opened his eyes.

He saw a littered walkway between two buildings, run-down, neglected. Cans and papers were scattered about, cracked stucco was scaling from the walls. There was the unmistakable odor of urine. Not a pleasant place to walk through, much less, to spend the night.

Did he live here?

Curiosity was waking in him. Suddenly there was much he did not know. He must belong here, yet in his mind there seemed a shadow of something else, of somewhere else. He ran his hand slowly over his face and his beard told him he had not shaved for a long, long time. His mouth tasted foul and dry, as if he had not eaten since he last shaved. He didn't think he was really hungry. He felt tired still, and his muscles and joints were aching. A definite odor was rising out of his clothes, which badly needed washing. When He looked down at the back of his hand he saw that dirt was ground into his skin and his fingers seemed stained and neglected. *I should stir myself, get something to eat and drink.*

Slowly he pulled himself to his feet, steadied himself, and began to mosey along the passageway. He came to the end of the walkway and moved stiffly and carefully down cracked and broken steps to a sidewalk below, emerging from between buildings onto a downtown street.

He looked around. Nothing looked familiar, though he believed it should. He tried to remember which way to go. On impulse he turned left and ambled forward, paying little attention to where he was going.

He shook his head, as if that would clear the confusion. There was something about himself he must know. At the intersection he looked up and down to be sure no speeding car would endanger him as he crossed.

He wandered on. One block. Another. Still another. He stopped. It was, he decided, a beautiful day. The sun was bright, the air was clear, and he was alive. He pulled his shoulders back and found it didn't require attentive effort to keep them so.

There is no excuse for my slouching.

That had to stop.

He lengthened his stride and began to swing his arms. It felt good to stretch his muscles and feel sidewalk sweep under him at a respectable speed.

This was how I walked when I was young. Then I always walked this way. When and why did I change?

There was that menacing, unspoken query gnawing on him just out of reach in the back of his mind. He would feel better when he had some food, he told himself. Not drink. He wondered if yesterday he might have wanted a bottle. There seemed no hint of thirst in his throat. Except for coffee. He longed for steaming black coffee.

Suddenly, he was hungry after all: thirsty and hungry. He wanted coffee and eggs, with ham, toast, and potatoes; with good strawberry jam such as Jan made every year.

Jan?

A name had come to him, a name that seemed somehow natural and important. Who was she? A person named Jan. A woman. He tried to picture what Jan might look like, the kind of person she would be. The name seemed familiar and special, the only name he had so far remembered.

He had to find some other names.

That was the threatening question. His own name. It was important. *My name is*–he tried hard, but could only almost remember. Maybe if he wouldn't try so hard it would come to him. He tried to stop thinking about names and to think only about walking in the sunshine and how good it felt.

Jan. The name brought him no pictured face, but it did bring a feeling of deep peace and warmth. Whoever she was, she was someone special to him. Maybe she had left him and he was here as he now was because of her going. It hurt to think, and he felt discouraged. His thinking produced only more questions without answers. His stomach was now insistently asking one thing: where and when food might be. He felt in his pockets and found them empty. He had no money. You could not live without money. Maybe he would find something to eat when he got where he was going.

He came to the end of another block and this time he saw a red light glowing at him from the fixture on the post on the opposite corner. He waited for the signal. It was an excuse to stop, to look around and get some idea where he was going. Still, nothing looked familiar. He peered ahead at the next block, with its row of run-down stores, shops, and service places seemingly stretching out to a ramshackle infinity. On the opposite corner was a large gray-stone building. It seemed to reach up above the whole neighborhood, and he looked absently at the cross that stood at the pinnacle of the steeple silhouetted against the sky. It was an old church, one that had obviously seen better days but still appeared open, attended, and ready for business this bright morning. The metal gateway leading to the door marked "Office" was clearly unlocked and ajar.

That building held promise for him, he decided. Something about it was drawing him to it. Was this the place where he came for help, food and drink? Or was there something more there, something he could almost remember, something not quite forgotten?

The signal winked green and he made his way quickly across to where the gate of promise beckoned. He went up the steps, through the door and into the hallway. It smelled the way a church should smell, an odor of quiet sanctity and deep serenity. To the right was a glass door leading into the church office. He looked in, careful to avoid being noticed. Several women were there, standing, sitting and talking in young, loud voices. He slipped quickly beyond that doorway and down the hall toward the double oak doors bearing the worn brass sign, "Sanctuary." He would come back later to this office, when the in-house business had subsided and someone would be free to deal with a needy outsider. Right now, he felt a longing to go into that place with the promising name. He hoped the door was not locked.

It wasn't. The door swung open with a gentle squeak, and he was in the dim, high-vaulted auditorium, looking down the aisle toward pulpit and altar and large stained glass windows. The something in him that had begun to stir this morning was at last rejoicing. This was all familiar.

He looked carefully at the altar and the pulpit and around the walls. It felt familiar. Was this church known to him, or did he feel this way about being in any church? He looked again at the scarves hanging from the pulpit and lectern, and covering the altar.

Purple. Judging from the weather outside it must be Lent: late March or early April. No palm branches around, so perhaps Palm Sunday was still to come.

Lent. Another name.

But now he was using lots of names. These things were very familiar to him.

Pulpit and lectern and chancel— the nave, the narthex, the pews, the baptismal font; he named them as he turned slowly, surveying the room. Somehow, this seemed so usual.

The thought of Palm Sunday felt right.

"And the people took branches of palm leaves and went forth to meet Him and cried, 'Hosanna. Hosanna. Hosanna.'" He uttered his first sound, his voice hoarse from lack of use. He imagined this room filled with worshippers, reliving the triumph of that ancient day in Jerusalem. He walked up the aisle slowly, savoring the feelings of this holy place.

That is a good pulpit, he thought. Well placed for being seen, sturdy and equipped for effective preaching. He looked to see if there were any notes, or maybe a bulletin, left there from last Sunday. Perhaps they would tell him what day it was or year it was, and what this city was. Possibly they would start to supply those answers he needed so desperately.

Yes—the question that had been lying in wait for him at the back of his whole consciousness was now out in the open: Who and what was he?

He stepped into the pulpit and looked inside and beneath the reading stand. The custodian had done his work well. There was nothing left to tell him what had happened last Sunday, nothing but a hymnal and a Bible and the pulpit itself. He stood and looked out over the empty pews. As bright as the sunshine was outside, it was dark in here; but it was a darkness that could not be described as gloomy. It was restful. The shadows that filled so much of the space before him seemed to be shades of the joy and love of those who regularly came here. Much spoke to him of faith. He braced his arms on either side of the pulpit and leaned forward over the desk.

It would be easy to preach from this pulpit to the congregation in this place. It would not be the best appointment in the conference, and you would never be elected bishop from such a church, but the people would be sound and the work solid and worth doing. He glanced back at the pipes that towered above his head in the wall behind the pulpit.

A pipe organ: no question of it. Good. That was usually the best sound for worship. Much could be said for other accompaniments, even the guitar, but for the whole church to sing the great old hymns required the voice of a good organ and a skilled organist.

He looked up at the balcony. It was probably unused, except at Easter. Even if the church were only half filled, it would be enough to call forth a good sermon from any preacher worthy of his calling. In his mind's eye he began to see them sitting expectantly in their pews, ready to hear the teaching he might bring from the Lord. He threw his head back, closed his eyes, and uttered the words of Ascription:

5

"In the Name of The Father, and of Jesus Christ The Son, and of The Holy Spirit. Amen."

A voice answered him out of the shadows at the back of the auditorium, "Hey you, what do you think you are doing up there?"

He was silent as he sought for an answer and found one: "I believe, sir," he replied slowly and clearly, discovering the truth in himself with every syllable, "I believe I just found out who I am."

TWO

◆

Without warning, music harshly intruded upon and shattered Jan's dream. She realized almost at once that it was her clock radio, demanding this new day should begin. Jan reluctantly agreed this was timely, right, and necessary. "But please," she thought, "not just yet." She wanted to dwell on the echoes of her dream and how it had made her feel, just a little bit longer.

This dream had been so different from any of the others.

So she continued to lie there, running over in her mind the unusual and still vivid episode that had been dispersed by her abrupt awakening. In it she had found herself standing at what seemed to be a kitchen sink, looking out of a window across a lawn at a walkway of pink cement, a short set of steps with a black enamel iron railing, leading to an ornate front door. She felt she had been washing dishes, and was vaguely conscious of the foaming warm water still there beneath her hands; but she was more interested in the building just across that stretch of lawn and the sidewalk than in what she had done or was about to do. She had an unexplained impression that the building next door was a church. She could not see any sign or symbol to confirm this or to tell where it was or what kind of church it might be, but she was sure that's what it was. And she knew somehow, *he* was over there, somewhere inside.

She had no name for *him*, and had never been able to decide what to call *him*, other than just "he." She knew in this she was different from other women. Everyone had dreams, but her dreams were always vivid and memorable and were always about the same man. To her waking life *he* was a stranger, but she had been dreaming about *him* as far back as she could remember.

7

But this time was different. She had not actually seen *him* at all. Instead, she had seen a place where *he* was and that, if it existed, she would be able to identify if she ever saw it again. The rose-colored concrete of the broad walkway, the gleaming black enameled iron railings beside the broad steps, the ornate double doors—every detail was etched in her mind.

She shook off her preoccupation, reminding herself it was past time to shower and get dressed. And she would need to take special care with her preparations today, for she had agreed to go out to dinner with Jerry when the library hours were over.

In the shower, as the water streamed over her, she thought about Jerry. He was the latest in what she had to acknowledge was a long parade of eligible and suitable bachelors. She had never lacked for male admirers, but here she was, approaching middle age–with that old biological clock running down–and still an old maid. Maybe this time she would finally be able to forge a relationship that would lead to the altar and to what she thought of as a normal life. Lots of women could, would (and, perhaps, should) decide to live their lives without a husband. Jan understood this and had no quarrel with it, but she had never been tempted to include herself in their number. Truthfully, there was nothing she wanted so much as to be married to the right man.

As she stepped out of the shower she caught sight of herself in the mirror. She had to admit she had no excuse to still be single. Five foot six in height, a shade under one hundred twenty-six pounds, with a face framed in golden hair and what she judged to be a normally attractive shape, many men in the past had described her in whispers as "lovely, beautiful." Yet she remained still on the shelf, unclaimed.

The right man. Again and again, it had seemed to her a "right" man was interested in her, paying court to her, even standing right beside her, awaiting the tactical moment to propose. But then she would always dream–of *him*. And those dreams were so rich with feeling, so warm and loving that the power and promise of the waking relationship would flicker and fade in her heart. The men were almost never the problem; she was. She would find herself suddenly convinced this was another relationship that just could not work. Compared to *him*, this was not Mr. Right after all. She had still to wait.

Jerry was a good man: thoughtful, polite, ambitious, well-spoken, successful. He would be as good a husband as a dozen of his predecessors would have been. Something was wrong with her. Otherwise, why must she be doomed to spend her life waiting for a phantom of her nights who never appeared to her waking eyes?

As she was putting on her jacket she thought back to last night's dream. It had, in truth, felt different. This time *he* had not put in an appearance. Was *he* in fact beginning to recede? She could hope almost that things might at last be changing for her. Was this a good omen for Jerry?

Jan closed and locked the apartment door behind her. She would just have to wait and see.

Out of the shadows at the back of the church and down the center aisle hurried a slim angular man, dressed in brown corduroy trousers and a blue flannel shirt. John thought it unlikely that he was the pastor, yet he spoke with authority. Probably the custodian, he thought. Part of his duties, of course, would be to deal with drunks and derelicts who might wander into the church. That was the duty he was carrying out now. How could he be made to believe that this time he should make an exception?

John rubbed his hand over his bristling face and was again aware of the strong smell from his rumpled and filthy clothing. That was what he was, a "street-person"—a "bum" or "tramp" in an older vocabulary—homeless, destitute, perhaps alcoholic; a wanderer in his own private hell, lost and alone in the midst of the living.

But he had not always been so. He knew that now. In the last few moments he had remembered enough to see and understand the heights from which he had fallen. He could now speak a name that was his own. Again, he thought of Jan and knew at once she was his wife. What more could he remember? Fragments of pictures began to rush together in his mind's eye. He had been respected and had fallen. Much was still hidden in darkness. Still, there was the faintest glimmer of light in the thought, "Might I yet climb back up?"

"You've no business in here, neighbor." The custodian was speaking with quiet firmness. "What you want is the City Rescue Mission. It's three blocks down, and a block over..."

That would be somewhere close to the place where he had started this morning.

Strong fingers grasped his elbow and began to move him into the chancel and down the aisle.

"The Pastor... I want to see your Pastor," he stammered.

"He's very busy this mornin', and there's nothin' he could do for you. As I said, your best bet is the City Rescue Mission. All of the churches raise funds to help folks, but then they do all the givin' of 'em. I'm sure you'll get help there..."

Unless he did something quickly he would be outside in the bright morning, and an all-important chance would have been missed. He had to see the senior minister, to talk out the things springing up in his mind, and find out the details of where and when he was emerging from darkness.

He stopped, wrenching his elbow from the grasp of his escort. "No, I must see the pastor. You must believe me. This is an emergency."

The movement and words were met with hard annoyance: "Just what kind of *emergency* can it be? Doesn't it boil down to a hand-out—without havin' to work for it, if possible? Some special reason why you should be treated to a meal or housing or a bus ticket, an' maybe a few bucks, for some tough situation you have thought up?"

He looked evenly back into the gray forthright eyes. "Maybe I will need all of those things, but right now what I need more are answers to a lot of questions. This is a really 'tough situation', as you put it. I am an ordained minister, but I have no idea where I am or how I got here."

The other stepped back, shaking his head, and slowly ran his eyes deliberately up and down John's frame, beginning with the run-down sockless shoes and ascending to his matted and filthy hair. "Well, that's a new one, for sure. A minister, now?"

"That's right, and right now I'm as puzzled as you are. I don't know what city this is, or the day of the week or time of the month—not even the year. There are more things I don't know than things I do."

"Well, at least that's original. But you're still goin' to have to go three blocks down and a block over. You can tell them your story. They can answer any questions that need answerin' and give you what you deserve. I can't help you, and Doctor Braddock..."

"You really don't believe me, do you?" John broke in.

The head shook slowly. "You say you're a minister—or were. Well, ok, Reverend. Would you believe a story like this told to you in your church?"

A good and fair question, he thought. He wasn't sure he could truthfully answer. He said desperately, "At least I'd want to check it out—if my staff would give me a chance to hear about it."

They had now emerged through the doors from the sanctuary into the hallway and were walking past the office. This might be his one chance. Quickly, he again tore himself from the custodian's grasp and bolted through the doorway, swinging the heavy door back against the wall with a crash. The startled secretary looked up from the patterned overlay of papers she was working on. Behind him he sensed the anger of a temporarily outflanked custodian.

"I must have an immediate appointment with Doctor Braddock."

Her round, bespectacled face looked past him at the gestures and expressions of his shadower. "Our pastor is very busy with important things today. Are you sure it wouldn't be better for you to go to the City Rescue Mission, at Tenth and 'B' Streets? That's three blocks down, and one block over. They..."

"I am an ordained minister, I need counseling and professional assistance, and I am asking—pleading—for an appointment with your pastor at the earliest convenient moment." He knew the firmness in his voice contrasted harshly with his disheveled appearance. He wondered what his own secretary, Virginia, might have done if this situation had arisen in his own church office. (*How long ago was that?*)

A shadow of doubt crossed her face, a hint of perplexity. "I really don't know what to say. Does Doctor Braddock know you? Would he recognize your name?"

He looked down without answering. After a moment he shook his head and replied in a low voice: "No, he would not. As far as I am aware, I have never heard of him. I doubt he has heard of me. An hour ago I couldn't remember who I was. Now I am beginning to recall many things; just how many, I don't know myself. I need a colleague to help me and it is a matter of extreme urgency for me and my wife, to say nothing of my church. I really am an ordained United Connectional minister, regardless of how I appear..."

While he had been speaking, a door on the side of the office behind him opened soundlessly; and a man in his late thirties, of medium height and trim build with thinning brown hair and dressed in gray trousers and a light blue clerical shirt, now stood in the doorway.

"You say you are... were... a United Connectional pastor? When and where was that?"

He looked at the newcomer and knew at once this was the man he had been asking to see. "Doctor Braddock, I am Reverend John Lewis Masters, ordained elder in the California Conference of The United Connectional Church, appointed most recently to the church in

Centerville, California. How long ago that was, I'll need help to find out."

The younger cleric looked levelly at him for a long moment. "Come in here, brother," he said, gesturing his invitation, "Let's see if we can get to the bottom of this." They stepped into the book-lined study, the door closed behind them, and John was motioned to a comfortably worn leather chair.

"Please sit down." The clergyman seated himself behind a large and alarmingly neat walnut desk.

"I must apologize to you for my condition. This morning I woke up in an alleyway between two buildings not far from here, looking as you see me. I have no idea how or when I got there. Before this morning I don't seem to have known who I was. I really didn't remember much of anything until I came into your sanctuary and got into your pulpit. Then things began to come back to me. I really have no idea what has happened to me, nor how long I've been this way."

A shrewd glance from the eyes behind the desk was followed by a question, "Perhaps you would tell me something; what are the 'Synoptic Gospels' and why are they so called?"

A test question. John found himself smiling for the first time since he had awakened this morning. "The Synoptic Gospels, Matthew, Mark, and Luke, are so called because they tell essentially the same Gospel story and see the life of Jesus with the 'same eye', in contrast with the Gospel of John, a Gospel concerned mostly with Christ's ministry in Samaria and Judea."

"And which Gospel was written first?" (*No hint either of approval or disapproval.*)

"Well, back in seminary I was taught it was the Gospel of Mark, but that was before Butler and Farmer and the rest had pointed out the fallacies in the 'two-document' theory of Streeter and established the credentials of Matthew as the earliest Gospel."

Suddenly Jim Braddock was grinning. "You sound like a preacher to me. Maybe a panhandler could answer the first question, but it takes something of a scholar to answer the second one the way you did. I have to admit I have Farmer's book but haven't gotten around to reading it yet. Let's see if we can't begin to figure this out. Can you tell me the last thing you remember?"

John rubbed his hand over his face thoughtfully, then spoke slowly: "It was what we used to call 'Passion Sunday,' two Sundays before

Easter. I was preaching from the lectionary on John eleven, the raising of Lazarus. I know the date was April first because I had inserted a crazy notice in the bulletin as a joke for my congregation. Sunday, April first—yes, I am sure that is the last real date I can remember."

There was a sudden hush. Something had clearly gone wrong. The other was staring at him without a hint of amusement.

"But April first was only last Sunday."

THREE

---◆---

Silence. He took a quick breath, then a deep one. What could he say? Braddock had shown every sign of believing him until just this moment. Now? Well, obviously what he had said was impossible. *And I was so sure these memories coming back to me were real, were true.* He again ran his fingers over the beard on his cheeks.

"What day of the week is it today?" he finally asked softly.

"This is Tuesday, April third. It is now nine forty-seven, Mountain Daylight Time."

John's eyes were drawn to the large calendar on the wall, clearly indicating this was indeed the year he thought it was. It took him a moment to comprehend what had just been said to him. "Mountain time. I'm not in California?"

"No. Colorado. Denver, Colorado."

John shook his head. "And I didn't grow this beard, ripen these clothes, get in this condition, and travel a thousand miles in two days. Those memories of mine just can't be as good as I thought they were. Yet, I was so sure... Could I have been confused? Maybe I saw a paper in the last couple of days that recalled to me when April Fool's day fell on Sunday. Last year, maybe, two years ago. There has to be some explanation."

The pastor reached into his desk, rummaged about for a moment, and pulled out a cardboard device with dials and numbers, quickly manipulating it. "Perpetual calendar," he muttered in explanation. "Last time was six years ago. Before that it was eleven years ago. Could it have been then?"

"Six years? No, I was still in the church in Henley then. My

14

memory is definitely of a time since then, because five years ago I was appointed to Centerville. I would have sworn it was last Sunday. But that's obviously impossible."

"If that is what you remember, stick by it. But in the past five years, this is the first year April first has fallen on Sunday."

"Then how did I get here, looking like this? After Sunday morning I draw an absolute blank. I seem to recall standing in my pulpit, preaching as usual, and then... well, I don't remember anything more. I simply cannot picture finishing the sermon, singing the hymn, pronouncing the benediction, or going to the door. I don't recall speaking to anyone after the service or going into the coffee hour in the Social Hall. I don't remember going home or what Jan had ready for our dinner... And I know nothing of yesterday at all."

Doctor Braddock was obviously sincere in his interest again. "What can you remember before the sermon? How are your memories of Saturday night?"

"Pretty good. I spent the morning finishing my income tax returns and getting 'em in the mail. There were several phone calls... Oh, my Lord—a funeral—I was to have had a funeral this morning." He shook his head in real pain over this latest lapse in his behavior that had just become evident. He was letting down a family that had trusted him.

"These things are all real for you; you can really picture them happening?"

"Oh yes. I can't doubt they are true and are real memories. The family's name is Ferguson. It was the husband, Henry, age eighty-three, who had died. I talked with his widow and their son Saturday night. I spent over an hour with them, listening to how they felt about him and encouraging them to talk until their feelings came through; making sure they felt free to grieve."

The man behind the desk reached for a small paper-bound booklet. "Will you tell me again about your text for Sunday?"

It was a relief not to think about that ruined funeral for a moment. "Yes. It was the eleventh Chapter of John, the raising of Lazarus. Here the Pharisees were looking far off to the end of history when resurrection would take place on the Day of the Lord, and Jesus says to them 'I am your resurrection.'"

"That fits, John," the other broke in. "John 11:1-45 is the Gospel Lesson in the Consultation on Church Union Lectionary. I haven't been using it because I have had a special Lenten series, but it sounds as if you did."

"Yes," he agreed slowly, "I do—I did—use the COCU Lectionary."

"And this confirms your story. Look, John–if this was some kind of dream or hallucination cooked up by an alcoholic mind, you wouldn't know the Scripture to use..." A shadow of doubt flickered across his face even as he spoke.

John saw it and acknowledged it by finishing it himself: "....nless I am some kind of crafty con artist who has prepared himself to take in the local church leaders in some scam."

"I don't really believe that for a moment. I don't see, for one thing, how it would pay off. And more to the point, I think you believe what you are telling me." He rose again from his chair behind the desk and walked to the window.

"I'll be frank. I cannot see any way what you have told me can possibly be true; and I also cannot bring myself to believe you are lying to me or deceived about yourself. I've never been in any situation like this before in my life." .

The erstwhile indigent leaned forward, rubbing the back of his head. "I can't begin to blame you. I have to believe my memories, but I cannot see how I can be a run-down, seedy, unwashed has-been two days after I was last functioning effectively as a successful, well-groomed and well-thought-of pastor."

Suddenly he stood up, walking to stand beside his colleague and host. "To be honest, I've been entertaining some pretty fantastic ideas in the last few minutes. You know, far-out stuff, on the occult fringe—transmigration of souls, out of body experiences, things like that. But it can't be. This is me, in my body. I know it, even if I can't explain it, Doctor Braddock."

"John, please call me Jim. How can you be so sure?" Obviously some such ideas had occurred to Jim Braddock too.

"This scar on my left forearm; I got it trying to ride my bike too fast down a steep hill in a rain storm when I was fourteen. This is my body."

The pastor put his arm lightly on the other's shoulder. "Well there is a test that we must try, and right now. We have to call California and find out about that funeral service. If it is pending and they are unaware of what has happened, whatever the explanation, they deserve to know now in time to make other arrangements. You are not going to make it for that service."

"By now they are already painfully if not angrily aware of that fact," John Masters said slowly.

"Maybe not. It is just now nine o'clock in California. You said the service was scheduled for ten. Do you recall the name of the mortuary?"

"Sure. Murphy and Hayes. Centerville. The number is... I think it is..."

"Never mind about that. My secretary can use what we have." He flipped the intercom switch.

"Charlotte, please get me the Murphy and Hayes Funeral Home in Centerville, California. Let me know when you have them on the line." The box acknowledged the instruction in muffled feminine tones.

"What are you going to tell them? I don't know what to say. The pastor they trusted to help them deal with this loss and emptiness in their lives is off in a city half a continent away, looking and smelling like a skid-row bum. I have always lived with a terrible fear I might sometime, somehow, let a family down, but this is far worse than anything I have ever imagined. I just don't know how to begin to explain..."

The intercom interrupted imperiously. "Your call is ready, Doctor Braddock. It is Mister Hayes on the line."

The pastor picked up the phone. "Mr. Hayes, this is Doctor James Braddock at Saint Matthew's Presbyterian Church in Denver, Colorado. Do I understand you have a service scheduled for a Henry Ferguson this morning? Reverend John Masters is to officiate, I believe, and..." He paused and listened intently.

After a long moment he replied quietly, "Oh, I see. Yes. Well, thank you very much. That does give me the information I need. I trust you will have a good day." Slowly he slipped the telephone back into its cradle.

He sat looking at it for what seemed like a full minute before glancing up. "That funeral is scheduled for this morning: Henry Ferguson, age eighty-three. The pastor of the local United Connectional Church is to conduct the service."

"Then why did you hang up? Why didn't you tell them I couldn't..." The look on Dr. Braddock's face stopped him in the midst of his anguish.

"The pastor's name is Ben Richardson. He, of course, is officiating. Your name meant nothing at all to him."

FOUR

♦

Another long silence. Then, as if a dream was ending, the man calling himself John Masters slumped in his chair, burying his head in his hands. He felt himself drifting slowly once again into that blackness from which he had only just begun to emerge. He had been so sure he knew who he was: Reverend John Lewis Masters, Elder and Pastor in the California Conference of the United Connectional Church, serving in his fifth year as Pastor of the century-old congregation in Centerville, a thriving small city in the foothills of the Sierras. Memories had been coming back to him in bursts of image and feeling. He had been so sure.

And Braddock had obviously been open to the possibility that what he was saying was the highly improbable truth. It was important he should believe, for John would have to have massive and timely help given if he was to return to his pulpit with a minimum of scandal and disruption.

Scandal. Yes, here was a key word. How had he awakened today to find himself in this condition, in this place? The memories that had been returning were all of last week, in his own church, with his wife and friends. He had no memory at all of yesterday, or of the events that had cast him up upon the streets of Denver, a filthy, homeless vagrant.

Jan.

As he recalled her name now he not only knew her to be his wife but pictured her beautiful face, her warm smile, her long golden hair. What must she be thinking of all this and how could he explain to her what had happened? If Ben Richardson was Pastor now, where was Jan? She would at least be able to tell him the observed details of

18

his disappearance from Centerville, and how he had been replaced so quickly.

Quickly? Instantaneously.

No one was ever replaced in a church in three days. It was unthinkable. There had to be some other explanation. Of course, there was. All of the problems arose from the memories that had come back to him this morning: memories so out of keeping with every single bit of evidence that had so far been put forward. Obviously his recollections could not be trusted.

If he was not in fact the pastor of that California church, who was he? He could offer no reason for Jim Braddock to believe him. His story sounded like the fantasy of an alcoholic slyly working up to his next binge.

Suppose I am not the Reverend John Lewis Masters. My memories actually might be a kind of alcoholic delusion, like pink elephants and delirium tremens. Perhaps this was the result of some fantastic transference involving a story I once read, or some person I once knew. I might be nothing but a poor sodden tramp whose mind is trying to hide in the day dream of a good life that exists only in my imagination. If this is the case, the best thing I can do would be to get out of this pastor's study and back to the streets and doorways from which my mind has tried to escape. If only I could remember yesterday. If only there were some recollections other than the impossible ones connected with my supposed clerical life. If only...

A strong hand gripped his shoulder reassuringly. Jim Braddock's voice said quietly, "It isn't as bad as it sounds, John." The minister had risen from his chair and come around the desk to stand behind him.

John did not look up. "How could it be worse?......ave not been... lying to you. I really believed everything I told you. I really think... thought... I was a United Connectional minister. I don't understand what has happened to me, or who I could really be, if..."

"John, I believe you. I am sure you are telling me the truth. Stop and think." The pastor walked to the other side of the room, tolling off on his fingers each point as he made it.

"You knew the name of the man in California whose service is being held this morning; you knew his age, the name of the mortuary where the service is being held. How would you know all of this if you were a 'Denver down-and-out'er?' And no matter how you look, you don't sound like an alcoholic, and I can't see what this ploy would get

19

you if you were. You sound to me like a minister who finds himself in a totally perplexing situation. I am as baffled by the whole thing as you are, but I have to believe you and think we will find the solution."

John felt the darkness again recede. He looked up into the earnest face of his new-found friend. "I guess you're right. I am glad someone is able to reason clearly, because I've had about all I can manage."

With an air of sudden decision, Jim Braddock drew a chair up facing him, and sat down. "Let's see if we can't find some handles for this situation. What was your seminary and class?"

"Hilltop School of Theology, Berkeley. Graduated twenty years ago. Master of Divinity."

"Hilltop. There's a good friend of mine who got his degree from Hilltop maybe twenty-three, twenty-four years ago. He might be able to give us some real help in getting you back on solid ground and answering questions about yourself."

"That would have been just before my time, but we would know lots of people in common. What church is he serving?"

"None. He dropped out of the ministry several years ago to take a job as an insurance executive."

"Many were doing that a few years back. Some do it even now." John again brushed his hand over his bristling beard. "Can't help wondering if that might not be what part of me was trying to do that got me into this mess."

The younger man reacted quickly. "Were you tempted to get out? Were you under stress—a lot of stress I mean?"

"Not as far as I am aware. Oh, I've had my moments, of course; thinking about doing something else—something from nine to five that would pay more, in keeping with my education and experience—who hasn't had those thoughts? But most of the time I remember finding my work challenging and a rewarding adventure. I really have no regrets over being called to the ministry."

"It was a 'call' then for you; not a 'vocational decision' when you were 'recruited'?"

"No, it was a real call. It wasn't my idea to become a preacher, and only the conviction that God wanted it and would make it possible for me made it at all thinkable." As he was speaking he realized that probably now all that was changed.

Jim Braddock pushed back his chair in sudden decision. "Well, it's getting late and we must start to deal with your situation. First things first. I want you to go out to the kitchen and get a cup of our coffee and some of the rolls my secretary brought in for us this morning. That should tide you over. Meanwhile I'll have her make arrangements for a motel room, and have her husband fix you up with the some clothes, a razor and the necessary toilet articles. Feel free to make any phone calls you feel like making from your room. I have some appointments I must keep today. Charge your lunch to the church at the coffee shop next to the motel, and when I can, I'll be in touch as to when we can go and talk with your fellow-seminarian. Maybe we can have dinner with him tonight. Meanwhile, you get cleaned up and rested and feeling yourself again. We have a mystery to solve."

John stood up. He took Jim Braddock's extended hand and shook it with a grip made strong by gratitude. He knew now he had come to the right place. And he discovered he was able to stand fully erect, and felt surprisingly well.

FIVE

♦

The steamy after-shower air comforted John as he wrapped himself in the towel, fastened it with a knot, and sorted through his new toilet kit before for shaving. He felt eager to get his physical body back into its accustomed condition; scrubbed, freshened, and well-groomed. The stinking clothes now lay on the floor and would be disposed of as soon as he was dressed and could take them to the motel trash bin.

He spread the shaving cream over his moist face with practiced ease and began to deftly scrape away at the long whiskers with this latest multiple bladed marvel of the razor-maker's art. His remembered face began to emerge in the misty mirror. He could see nothing in his face to indicate any extended time of hardship or debauchery. He felt sure he had last done this only day before yesterday in the upstairs bathroom of the parsonage in Centerville.

However, the growing mass of long whiskers threatening to clog the drain were not the result of a mere three days of growth. This was a major discrepancy he could not explain. Nothing about his physical state could be accounted for, assuming his memory of his last day in California was accurate and this present time was not only part of the same year, but the same month and the same week.

Once again he searched his memory for his last remembered experience prior to his awakening this morning, and the menacing confusion that followed. That Sunday morning had begun with the usual chores of preparation and last minute crisis. Mrs. Brockner had come to his study to make arrangements regarding her daughter's June wedding in the church. The Godsen twins, scheduled to be the acolytes lighting the candles in the service, had not shown up for

Sunday school, so substitutes had to be found for them. He recalled the anthem the choir sang and the scripture lesson being read. He could remember the offertory being played and his arising and beginning to preach. But... what then? He could not remember standing at the door or any conversation in the coffee hour following the service. He could not even recall singing the final hymn. He could not call to mind the benediction used to close the service.

It was as if whatever had happened had taken place in mid-sentence somewhere in his sermon. Was there a shock, some blow—a vascular spasm or rupture in his brain? Maybe he was the victim of some sort of fugue, and his subconscious rebelled at the emotional pressures of now forgotten events and feelings. He must have bolted from his former life to take refuge here in an existence opposite in every detail to what he always valued. He did not think that could happen without his conscious mind knowing of it and remembering it

Once again he faced the possibility that his memories were not real at all, but rather delusions. He could not have been in his pulpit in California on Sunday and here, down-and-out with a month's growth of beard and richly seasoned clothes only two days later. Therefore those memories were false and totally untrustworthy. They were the product of a deranged mind, somehow driven past its ability to cope. He must be an alcoholic who for this moment was dreaming of what he might have been and how he might have lived; those dreams had clothed themselves in temporary garments of pretended reality.

Except—Jim was right. If that were the case, how would he know about the service for Henry Ferguson this morning and even the name of the mortician? He absolutely knew himself to have detailed knowledge about churches and ministry, the Bible and pastoral administration. The simplest and most logical hypothesis was not supported by the evidence when you looked at it carefully. The evidence seemed to indicate his memories were substantially true. The mystery of how they could be true stubbornly persisted and claimed the center of his concern.

He had no answer. It would take more time, more facts, and some help before it could be finally resolved.

He carefully touched up the last places on his face where any roughness remained, and plunged the razor into the scalding water under the spigot. He shook it to remove the droplets and placed it in its case. With the wash cloth, he wiped away the last flecks of lather. He focused on the mirror again and drew near enough to study his eyes.

No jaundice, no appreciable redness. He couldn't find any difference now between himself in this reflection and the man remembered from other mirrors.

He came out of the bathroom into the pleasant motel room that Jim had secured for him. There on the bed were the clothes brought by Hammond Black, Charlotte's husband. He repeated the names again to fix them in memory. Charlotte was Jim's secretary, and she was the one to whom he had been appealing when Jim Braddock first emerged from his study this morning. "Ham" was in the clothing business and it had not taken him long to leave his store, come to the church, size up the newcomer, and appear at the motel a few minutes after he registered with a complete outfit of new, good-looking clothes, and the other necessities.

He picked up the shorts and drew them over his naked body. John then luxuriated in the crisp cleanness of the shirt. The pants followed, creased and slightly stiff. He sat on the bed and put on socks and shoes, feeling rigid newness that would have to be worn away before they would become truly comfortable. He thrust the belt through the loops that circled his waist, and buckled it snugly. There, he was himself again.

For a long moment he sat perfectly still. Was he? Slowly he slid to the floor, turning to kneel beside the bed. He clasped his hands before him and bowed his head over them. Within himself he opened the windows of his soul and sought to feel the presence of God. His spirit rose to seek his Creator.

He began to pray softly, "Eternal God, I truly believe You are here. I thank You for Your Presence and Your love. I don't understand this situation in which I find myself, Lord. I can't imagine how I can be here and what this means. But I do claim Your promise that 'all things will work together for good to those who love You, who are called and submitted to Your purposes.' I entrust myself, my life, my ministry, my wife and friends—all things, to Your care. And so, Lord, I give You all the praise...." His voice trailed off into silence.

Within his deepest part he thought he felt words form: *Be at peace. All is in My keeping.*

For several moments he just let himself relish those words.

Had he truly heard God's answer, or was this his own mind responding with what he hoped and wished for; was this spiritual reality or self-deception? He wanted to feel sure it was the former, but he had been sure of so much already today. He knew the importance of faith and affirmation. So as he continued to kneel, he quietly said, "Thank you, Lord. Thank you, Jesus." and repeated this praise with a heart that began slowly to fill with peace.

At length he rose and began to walk around the room, seeking to amplify the joy he was striving to feel. His eye fell on the telephone beside the bed.

He had to make the effort; he had to know.

Would the motel permit him to make long-distance calls? He was sure it would be all right if they would let him do it. He picked up the phone and dialed the 1 followed by the area code and his own familiar home number. He listened as the phone began to ring. Would Jan be home on Tuesday morning? Didn't she have a prayer group today? The ringing stopped and a male voice said, "Yes?"

"May I speak to Jan Masters, please."

"Nobody here by that name."

"How long has she been gone?"

"Never heard the name before. You've got a wrong number."

He hung the phone up. He must have dialed wrong. He picked it up and dialed carefully again. It was answered almost immediately.

The same voice, "Yeah, what now?"

He hung up again. The church office would know where she was. Again he dialed a familiar number. A moment later he heard his secretary answer.

"Centerville Connectional Church... May I help you?"

"Can you give me Jan Masters phone number."

The answer came slowly. "Jan Masters, you say? I'm sorry, I don't know the name."

"Thank you," he said and hung up. He had one more thing to try. Carefully, he dialed Jan's cell phone number. Again, the sound of ringing. Then a very young girl's voice.

"I'm yours. Who's calling?"

"Isn't this Jan Masters' phone?"

"Sorry, guy. It's my phone but my folks won't let me tell you my name. Bye."

The mystery deepened now, but he clung to the hope that God was somehow in the midst of it. "Be at peace. All is in My keeping," he remembered. That would have to be enough. He had to believe those were truly God's words to him. God must be trusted to keep His word.

Then the phone rang.

SIX

♦

It was Jim Braddock.

"John, I got in touch with my friend, Wes, the fellow from Hilltop, and we're to have dinner with him this evening. How are things with you?"

John paused before answering. How could he not tell Jim about his "answered prayer" and about the confidence he now felt, even in the face of perplexity? How often the clergy fear to talk with each other about their faith and the experiences that come from God. Many times in the past he had shared some personal encounter with Christ with another minister, only to be met with embarrassed silence suggesting inability to believe in supernatural experiences. It was ironic but true: the people in his churches were often much more open to the witness of the personal power of God than were many of his colleagues. He really had no way as yet of knowing how Jim Braddock might react in this particular area.

"I feel much better and I look much better, so I guess things have to be looking up."

"And say, Wes tells me there's a man serving in the area who was a classmate of yours; a Ken Baker. Know him?"

"Sure I do. That's great. How can I get in touch with him?"

"Wes talked to him and told him he has someone he wants him to meet. He'll drive in this evening after a board meeting and will be at Wes' place. You'll see him there. Anything new you can remember?"

He thought of the phone call so recently concluded. He found himself still fearing Jim would stop believing him. Right now that risk had to be avoided.

"No, not a thing really, nothing that helps. There's no logical reason for it, but I feel a lot more confident than I did two hours ago."

"Well, keep up the good fight and I'll pick you up about five fifteen in front of the motel. 'Bye."

Slowly he laid the telephone back in its cradle. The evidence was building that something was seriously amiss with regard to his past in the California Conference. Tonight he would meet with Ken Baker and they should have a rousing good time reliving the three years they shared at Hilltop Seminary. Ken had lived down the hall in the dorm and they were best friends then. Their friendship had dried up in the years since because of the distance separating them. Ken rarely came back to the West Coast for the spring pastoral institutes and other special events held at Hilltop each year. Tonight should be an easy time—but then they should have known his name in Centerville. He would not have been surprised, under the circumstances, had he been told Jan Masters did not live there "any more." But to be told "no one by that name has ever lived here" he just could not understand. It bothered him more than anything else that had yet happened.

That "yet" was ominous. He had to prepare himself, to explore the possibilities in that word. There were several hours at his disposal to find out what he could about himself and his true situation. Right now it looked as if there were two possibilities:

First, some considerable time had passed since his latest memories of California, and he and Jan had been forgotten. Maybe the community memories were repressed because of the scandal of his conduct or disappearance. Perhaps those now living in the parsonage did not possess the knowledge available to the pastor and the church board. If this were the case, then current copies of the *General Minutes*, the national denominational directory, or even his own Conference *Journal* might not give any clues to his status or even his existence. But those *Journals* of a few years back would surely show him in his known appointments.

The second possibility was *impossible*, but had to be checked out in the light of the apparent enigma he was facing, that conference records would not show him at all. This, of course, could not be; but he would have to assure himself it was not. One copy of the denominational *General Minutes* or a Conference *Journal* from several years ago would set this question to rest, once and for all.

He opened the telephone directory and swiftly leafed through the pages until he came to the page headed "Rocky Mountain." Then he ran his hand down the page until it came to rest upon "Rocky Mountain Conference, The United Connectional Church," and the number to be called to reach the conference switchboard. He copied the number, then lifted the phone and dialed. After a moment the line came to life.

"Yes, may I speak to the treasurer's office, please." It would be most likely that the conference treasurer would keep a run of the *General Minutes*—he rather thought church law required it—"Yes, hello. I wonder if I might ask a great favor of you. Do you have a copy of the *General Minutes* for, say, 1998 or 1999? Yes, the *General Minutes*... I'll be happy to hold..." There was a long pause, then the sound of returning movement. "Good, you have? 1998? Fine. Would you please look in the index for Reverend John L. Masters and find the page where his appointment is listed? M-a-s-t-e-r-s, John—middle initial 'L'... you're sure? Would you please read the index to me?"

From the telephone the matter-of-fact feminine voice could be clearly heard, reading, "Marker, Francis; Martin, C.; Martin, H.; Martin, W.; Massermann, W.; Metcalf, H.; Merrywell, R. No sir, no Masters listed at all."

"Well, thank you. Thank you very much. Goodbye." The phone was back in its place. Somehow he had expected this inconceivable bit of information.

This mystery was not likely to be solved immediately. But there had to be someone, somewhere who remembered him. And just maybe that person would turn up tonight.

With Ken Baker coming, how not?

SEVEN

♦

Wes Hammetson's home turned out to be truly palatial to a man familiar only with church-supplied parsonages, and the dinner was sumptuous and well served. Wes was a graying, somewhat rotund man in his early fifties with a shy young daughter, the only one of his four children still at home (and briefly present during the dinner) and a quietly pretty wife, Ruth, who saw to it that good food appeared in amazing quantities at precisely the right intervals. She seemed to have someone working in the kitchen to help her, but whoever handled the behind-the-scenes arrangements went unseen and unheard.

John found himself watching Jim Braddock and his young attractive wife, Martha, with a deep sense of loneliness and loss. He remembered with aching anguish the telephone calls he had made this afternoon; and the conclusion, made inevitable by the second one, that the first was literally and precisely accurate. Where was his Jan? What had happened to her? What did she think had happened to him? Only the deliberately recalled inner word that he believed had come to him from God gave any comfort.

Dessert was now all but past and the pace of the meal winding down to make ready for the talk that was, after all, the purpose of the evening. He watched gratefully as his cup was filled again with fragrant, steaming coffee. He sipped the decoction from the French-roast custom-blended beans and noted once again that Wes was indeed living the good life.

He looked closely into the face of his host. Wesley Hammetson had graduated from Hilltop Theological Seminary the spring before his own enrollment there, so he could not expect to recognize or to be recognized by him. He searched his memories of times when he had

29

attended the Pastoral Institutes held yearly just before the beginning of Lent, to see if he could recall this face. In that framework it did seem familiar, but he could not be sure. Maybe they had seen each other, talked in groups together over coffee and cookies, or attended the same faculty seminars. There was no way of knowing. But here at least was someone who could accurately test his memories of the past and reveal to him any indications that they were in fact the laborings of an unbalanced mind. He found he was eager for the test to be taken and the result to become apparent—whatever it might be.

Wes drew out a pipe, loaded it with tobacco from a Morocco leather pouch, lit it with a special pipe lighter, and sat back in a cloud of pleasantly pungent smoke. "Well, Jim—Mr. Masters—what is this all about? What is this problem that you two are having and how can I help you?"

John spoke up quickly. "Please, Wes, call me John. I am the problem. I wonder if we might talk about Hilltop and our years there. You never knew me and I cannot honestly remember whether I have ever seen you before or not; you know how those Institutes were. I'd like to tell you about our seminary and answer any questions you have for me about it. The purpose of this is for you to establish in your own mind whether or not I graduated from Hilltop Theological Seminary three years after you did, as I truly believe. Then, when you are ready to render your decision and have told us what it is, we'll tell you why this is so important to us and especially to me."

Wes shook his head, smiling. "That's about as unusual a request as I have heard since I attended my last deacons' meeting. OK, Jim says this is serious and important, so lets 'have at it' as they say. Why don't you start out by telling me about Hilltop's campus as you remember it in the fall when you entered?"

"It is located on a hill just three blocks from the State University campus," John began, "a cluster of buildings around an open space of lawn criss-crossed by sidewalks. When I started that fall there were perhaps a hundred and twenty students. My first impression was that this was just one large and surprisingly harmonious family. The student body President that first year was Michael Inouye who was, I guess, the outstanding graduate of all my time at Hilltop. Straight 'A's', a brilliant preacher, and the most talented volleyball player I have ever seen."

Wes nodded agreement. "Yes, I remember Mike well. That was a mean spike he delivered. What about Wally Hamilton?"

The mention of that name brought back a vivid personality long unremembered for John. "I haven't thought of Wally for years. Nice guy, but given to practical jokes. He lived for 'em. He would go to any length to pull 'a good one' on us, especially the newly entered students. But Wally was just about the opposite of Mike: large, uncoordinated, and not really serious about his studies——at least to the point of achieving those outstanding grades, although he was intelligent enough. A great story around campus was of the weekend Wally found a senior's door unlocked and went in and replaced all the light bulbs with old-fashioned press-camera flashbulbs. Late Monday night when the senior returned I guess he thought the world was ending when he hit the light switch in his room."

Wes chuckled quietly. "Did they tell you I was that senior?"

"No, I don't think I heard the name of the victim, at least not to remember it."

"That is always the fate of us common folk: we pay the price for the genius of the Wally Hamiltons of this world, making their triumphs possible and being forgotten themselves in the process. What classes did you take that first quarter?"

"The usual basics: Introduction to Old Testament, Introduction to New Testament, The Religious Education of Children, Fundamentals of Preaching, Church Practicum. I guess for myself, as with most first year students, the most notable class was the Old Testament class with Wolters. That really broke us in right."

Wes was now grinning in shared remembrance. "He always delighted in scaring the entering students with his predictions. What did he say about your class?"

"The first day he came in, looked at us, and told us sixty percent of us would fail the quarter's work."

"Must have been a good looking bunch. He told us three-quarters of us would be repeaters, but we fooled him. Only about half actually didn't get recommended grades when the quarter ended."

John nodded. "I think he tried to shock us into diligence; perhaps two or three finally ended the quarter with a 'D' or an 'F'. But, boy, he did make us work. And he worked right along with us. I have never seen a professor before or since who insisted on grading his own papers and worked steadily until every paper had a typed commentary with grade, ready to be returned to the students at the next class session."

Wes drew on his pipe. "Did you live on campus?"

John crossed his legs easily. "Entirely, the first year. I was unmarried and had a job as youth minister with a church in Oakland. They paid me enough to drive back and forth several times a week from seminary. The next two years I had a wife and my own student church, and she lived out there in the old parsonage while I came in to seminary during the week and then returned to preach and run the church on the weekends. I lived upstairs in Witherspoon Hall and took my meals in the Co-op."

Wes leaned forward. "Which room in Witherspoon?"

"To be truthful with you, I don't remember the number. It was the room right at the head of the stairs as you came in the front door and went up the stairway."

"Anything unusual about it?"

"Not that I can think of."

"How about the pipes?"

John began to laugh. "Now I do remember something very unusual——haven't thought about that for years——those darned pipes would knock in an almost syncopated rhythm when the hot water was turned on to a slow trickle. Never did figure out why that happened."

Wes nodded. "" lived next door all three years, and heard that sound most mornings. Wally knew it would drive me up the wall and always set it to sound that way when he got up, three quarters of an hour before I did."

'It could be heard all over that end of the building. Wally didn't have the room in his last year, but he would come in whenever he could, asking to 'get some hot water' in a cup, and he would always set the faucet to do its thing. I caught on at last to what he was up to, but you couldn't be mad at the guy."

And so it went. They sat and enjoyed remembering together. An hour sped by as they talked together. Finally Wes paused, looked at John for a long minute, then turned to Jim Braddock with a smile. "I can't say, on the basis of this, whether our brother here actually got his degree from dear old Hilltop Teleological Cemetery, but I can tell you he was certainly privy to the secrets of that student body and did attend there. As we would say, 'he's a Hilltopper through and through'."

The confidence and good feeling in the room was palpable and warm.

At that moment the doorbell rang.

EIGHT

◆

From the direction of the front door drifted the sounds of an entering newcomer and the muffled greetings Ruth was uttering in welcoming Ken Baker. Ken was his classmate, now a necessarily neglected friend, with whom he had shared the experiences of those three years at Hilltop. They had first met at the Orientation week for new students before classes began and for the first two years they had lived in the same dorm, eaten most often at the same table in the Co-op dining room, and found themselves on work-details together as they served in doing their assigned part of maintaining and running the low-cost food service. Many an hour they had spent in the same lecture halls, and further had shared in discussing into the night what had gone on in those classrooms.

In the summer before their senior year Ken had married, and in consequence had been assigned a student church just a few miles from the church John served on weekends. So that last year they had usually driven back and forth together, with John stopping each Monday to pick Ken and his wife up, delivering them once again to church and congregation late on Friday afternoon. Now he could hear Ken's voice as Jim Braddock moved out to meet him in the hallway.

"What's this all about anyway, brother," came the well-remembered sound of a voice John had not heard since graduation. "Why were you so mysterious about wanting me to come here tonight? What was there that couldn't wait until I could come in to Denver and claim my reserved seat in your study?"

Braddock spoke slowly and with emphasis. "This is kind of an unusual situation, Ken. There is someone here I want you to meet and it is important you meet him tonight——important for his sake. This is an old friend of yours and, well, he has a problem. A problem neither he nor I can yet see the answer to."

"Well, I have to tell you I have done all the problem-solving I feel up to today, so I hope this is not going to be too difficult. I am beat." This last was uttered with cadence and emphasis.

"No, we really are not expecting you to give us all the answers, though we admit we can use all the help we can get. As a matter of fact, from what has already happened here tonight we could probably have avoided bothering you, because I feel sure what we are asking you to do has already been accomplished by Wes with his knowledge of Hilltop Seminary."

"It has something to do with that heresy hatchery?" Ken Baker jibed. "Well, nothing would surprise me, considering what I read in the Alumni Notes."

"This goes back a few years, because this man is a classmate of yours, a friend whom you haven't seen since graduation."

"Well, let's go in and let me see him. What's all the mystery?"

"That's just it. There are some things about this fellow neither he nor I can explain. If you had seen him as I did this morning, you would know how dubious his story sounded at first hearing."

John listened with mixed feelings to the clearly audible words and knew Jim Braddock was saying them loudly enough for him to hear them. Jim was setting the stage for the explanation of the problem and the involvement of Ken Baker in the solution, whatever it might prove to be.

But as he had listened to his classmate's voice, the last wisps of doubt and apprehension about his problem and situation had evaporated. Whatever the explanation finally turned out to be, there could be no doubt that now the solution would be found. He wanted to leap up and rush out into the hallway and initiate the embrace that would surely be Baker's spontaneous response as soon as he saw who it was that was awaiting him. He had to physically hold himself down and keep himself seated in the chair.

But he could not restrain himself from calling out: "Hey, out there. I only hear male voices. Don't tell me Baker didn't bring his lovely and talented wife, whom we all love and adore." Now Ken would know who it was that awaited him. How many times he had used that phrase with them both.

34

Ken Baker's voice sounded strangely puzzled. "Who was that, and what is this about? Everyone knows I have never been married." He stepped into the room and looked about.

Jim Braddock followed him in. "Well, Ken, here is your classmate and friend, John Masters."

Ken Baker, appearing just as he always had, looked right at John without any sign of recognition. "What are you talking about? I never saw this man before in my life."

NINE

♦

The silence and immobility of that moment seemed destined to last forever. John quickly looked from an obviously sincere and puzzled Ken Baker to a Wes Hammetson who looked as if he felt he had been made a fool of and showed signs of rising indignation and resentment. Then he shifted his gaze to an openly bewildered Jim Braddock. No one moved. No one spoke. Each was struggling with his own feelings, and clearly wondering what to do next, what to say, and what action to suit to the words that might come.

For John there had been only the flash of added pain and confusion as Ken Baker's words had struck home. But almost immediately that had been replaced by the wondering remembrance of an evening in the fall of their first year in seminary.

Across the bay in San Francisco a concert had been advertised, and John had decided a night of study could be sacrificed in order to attend it. Alvaro Marini, the internationally celebrated tenor, was scheduled to make one of his rare recital appearances outside of New York; and his voice and artistry were a special enthusiasm of John's at this stage in his life. He asked Ken Baker if he was interested in going with him, and they had agreed to seek inexpensive tickets and go. And so, on a chill fall night they had made their way across the Oakland Bay Bridge and found their way at last to Masonic Auditorium and the promised feast of vibrant song.

But the thing that made that night so important to remember was that the seats they had purchased were right next to those occupied by two young ladies who were students at San Francisco State College. In

36

the camaraderie of enthusiasm for the performer a conversation was begun while awaiting the start of the concert, renewed for its own sake during the intermission, and continued in a nearby coffee shop after the program had ended with the final encore. It was clear from the beginning that Valerie, the more vivacious and beautiful of the two, was attracted to Ken. John, as an engaged man, was pleasant and upheld his end of the conversation but also was amused to watch the chemistry of human relationships beginning to bubble in his unattached classmate. It was after midnight when they left the girls off at their dormitory, having first made plans for more communication and further meetings between Ken and Valerie. So they had gotten back very late to Witherspoon Hall, really too late in view of the early class that they both must attend the next day. But both went to their separate rooms agreeing it had been a splendid and worthwhile evening. Ken would have said so without any great singing at all, for something of obviously greater importance than German lieder and Italian arias was happening to him.

That had been the beginning. After that Ken would tell of evenings spent with Valerie, of things done and seen, and conversations shared. The couple were seeing each other quite as frequently as time permitted, and perhaps as far as Ken's courses were concerned, just a bit more. So it was with relief John heard the public announcement the following March of the planned marriage of Kenneth Baker and Valerie DuMennier. The wedding itself had taken place that summer.

In the fall the new couple had taken up residence in their first parsonage, in the church where Ken was the student pastor. Valerie had proved to be the ideal "preacher's wife"——a talented musician, beautiful, friendly, outgoing, and entirely devoted to her husband's calling. Often John had had reason to reflect on the wonders of providence and the love of God even in selecting the seating arrangements for concerts.

And now, in the face of that memory, he had heard Ken's claim to be unmarried. Ken had also said, with apparent honesty and sincerity, that he did not know John, had in fact never met him before. In a circumstance where this was true, then of course he would not have met Valerie, and would not have wooed and won and married her. He might well not be married. That realization was overwhelming and emotionally too big to digest, but it had to be faced and worked through.

John rose slowly to his feel, facing Ken Baker. "Ken, you say you do not know me, and you have never seen me before. Please understand

I am not doubting your word, but listen now to what I have to say. When you first came to seminary you were driving a black 1968 Ford two-door that gave the impression of being a very well-preserved car, and you had certainly given it the best of care. But three days after you arrived you were driving back up the hill to the parking lot when you blew the engine, and that car sat on the city street below the seminary for the next eight months, until it was finally towed away by the local gendarmes. You did not get enough for it out of salvage to pay the cost billed to you by the city for having it removed.

"Your first roommate when you arrived at seminary was Harley Whittaker, a rather quiet young chap from Oregon, who started his seminary career as a ministerial candidate from the Pentecostal Church of Faith. He was very outspoken in his criticism of the rest of the students and the faculty for their lack of credence in the particular doctrines in which he had been raised. But then, just before Thanksgiving, he packed his bags and his books and walked out of Hilltop while we were all at dinner. We did not see him again until our senior year when he turned up as a student in the nearby Unitarian seminary, wildly committed to a theology far more radical and modernist than anything any of our classmates could bring himself to believe.

"Your secret passion in those days was that butter-rum ice cream served at Benjy's Ice Cream Saloon down the hill toward the main gate of the University. When you could afford the money, time, and calories, you would eat a three- or even four-scoop dish. The night you passed the comprehensive exam we had to pass to graduate, you pigged out on a five-scoop 'mountain' and got rather ill. I do not remember ever going with you to that place again.

"You and Tucker McKnight spent an evening together investigating the possibilities of setting old hymns to new tunes, with the result that you found the meter of 'Jerusalem the Golden' fitted the tune for 'Tea For Two'. You then insisted on singing this horror for us all in our rooms, one by one, that night.

"Ken, you may not know me; I cannot explain that, but do you think I know you?"

Ken Baker was looking at John with obvious amazement.

"Everything you said was true, and I cannot imagine how you could know these things, since I honestly cannot remember you at all."

Wes Hammetson was also standing now. "You know too much about Hilltop Theological Seminary not to have been a student there sometime, and I don't see how you could get this information without having done what you said you've done; but why doesn't Ken know you?"

John's answer, whatever at that moment it might have been, was never heard, for a very distraught Ruth Hammetson appeared in the doorway. "Wes, please excuse yourself and get the car out. We've got to take Sarah to Emergency. She is terribly sick."

TEN

♦

Wes stayed his hurried departure in the doorway long enough to cover his responsibilities as the host to the other three men. "I hope we'll be back soon, but if we're not, treat the house as your own. My daughter is a severe diabetic. Her health is never really good and episodes like this can be very dangerous for her. I'm sorry to have to run out on you like this, but I'm sure you understand." He turned to go.

John knew he had to speak; the strong urge forming in the center of his awareness would not be ignored. "Wes, could we take just a moment now, before you go, to pray for Sarah?"

Wes was taken aback, and his face showed it. "Sure, why not?" He seemed about to bow his head in anticipation that John would begin the prayer.

"No, I mean, could we go to Sarah and pray for her and with her before she leaves. It will just take a moment."

Impatience acquiesced to good manners. "Of course. Come on."

Wes led the way to the family room where a very pale, obviously sick and helpless girl sat slumped in a chair, covered with a blanket and waiting to be scooped up in her father's arms and carried to the car. She did not even look up as the men entered the room. Wes led and came to stand behind the chair. John came second, and knelt on the child's left side, while the other two pastors stood on Sarah's right. Ruth stood in the doorway, poised to leave and not sure whether to be grateful or angry at the delay. She felt a gratitude to these ministers for the good thoughts involved in prayer, but was obviously convinced the best thing would be the activities of doctors and nurses, as quickly as possible.

Had it been left to either of the local active clergymen to begin the prayer, they would have expressed much the same idea; the blessings of God upon the child and upon the doctors who would be caring for her, and the strength and presence of God for the loved ones of the child in this time. Being professional church leaders, they believed in prayer and were thus always deemed automatically willing to pray for anyone at any time for any purpose; but they would not have felt prayer to be the highest priority at moments like this. When people asked for prayer, they felt constrained to pray and they believed God did do something good out of those prayers, perhaps in the intensification of the natural chain of events or the quiet strengthening of those distraught by worry. But this could have been effected just as well in the dining room after Sarah and her parents had left for the hospital, and would not have delayed what they felt was of first concern, the provision of expert medical assistance.

So they were both individually put off by the fact John Masters was now kneeling beside the child, and that he had placed his right hand on the child's head. John's voice began the prayer to which they were all supposedly giving their assent, in a voice that was strong without being really loud, and with an undercurrent of both urgency and conviction:

"Lord Jesus Christ, You promised that wherever two or three were gathered together, You would be here in our midst. We are your body, Lord, here to have You do through us what you did in our midst so long ago. We ask now that You will heal Sarah. Cause our hands to be Your Hand, and speak the word now that will make her entirely well. We thank You, Lord Jesus." John stopped speaking, and there was silence.

Silence. Each man prayed inside himself according to his own convictions, but after John's prayer none of the others felt the usual words to be adequate or to add anything. Wes became aware the hand he was resting upon his daughter's shoulder, in imitation of the placing of John's hand on her head, was growing warm. It seemed to him as if there was an unusual radiation emanating from the body of his child. It was not the clammy heat of high fever; rather it seemed somehow a clean, dry, healthy warmth and spoke goodness to his feelings but would have puzzled his understanding had he been seeking to understand.

John was clearly continuing to pray within himself. Slight movements of the lips and throat gave sign of sub-vocal prayer.

Ken Baker opened his eyes and looked down at the child. *If only I could see a prayer like this have some real effect.* The Wilsons, a

41

troublesome family of what he considered "fanatical believers," were always coming to him with tales of wonderful teachings heard and miracles observed that always ended in implications of needed change in his own understanding and ministerial style. They were gentle, sincere, and deeply disturbing, for they were so sure Christ acted now as the Gospels described Him acting. No amount of explanation about "the Gospels being the record of what the early church came to believe Jesus had done in keeping with a developing faith in Who he was" seemed to have any effect. These people could always tell some story cribbed from the latest of their growing collection of paperback books, or some account of a meeting they had attended or some spectacular narrative that they had heard from their even more fanatical friends, which would make it seem that such things happened and were still possible for believers today.

So Ken Baker found himself watching carefully. It seemed to him something was happening to the child. Her legs, previously drawn up in pain to her body, were now stretched out and at ease. The color seemed to be returning to her cheeks. She seemed to be relaxing all over. Could it be she had lost consciousness? He lifted his eyes to the others standing around the chair. None of them seemed to be looking; all eyes appeared closed. Perhaps Sarah had grown worse while they were praying, and only he had noticed this turn of events. He looked again at the stranger who claimed to be an old friend and who had demonstrated such knowledge of his seminary life. He was still praying, but his head was not bowed. Rather his face was turned up toward heaven, and his left hand was raised in supplication to God. If ever a man believed in what he was praying, Ken Baker decided, it was this John Masters. But was he doing good, or was every moment that passed a threat to the life of a girl who was very possibly now in a coma?

Jim Braddock also reflected critically on the wording and method of John's prayer. *Occasionally I have heard prayers like this before, and sometimes they seemed to have some real results. But we were taught in seminary to "be careful never to pray for the complete healing of anyone; always leave it finally and clearly in the hands of God to decide to heal or not to heal, and ask for strength and the working of patience, virtue, and the building of character in such afflictions that God does not heal; otherwise the faith of the one for whom you are praying may be permanently damaged when healing does not come."*

So Jim would not have prayed the prayer the man calling himself

John Masters had just prayed. As his sponsor at this meeting, he felt a bit betrayed that John would have behaved in quite this fashion, but he felt John's obvious sincerity and had to give the man credit for doing what he believed was right. Now Jim Braddock would have to undertake to repair whatever emotional damage this episode might cause for Ruth. (Wes, as a seminarian himself, could handle his own needs without help from still-active clergy.)

John broke the silence. "Thank You, Lord Jesus, for healing this child. We give You all the praise. Amen."

Now he rose, and the others shifted to let Wes get to his relaxed and seemingly sleeping daughter. But as Wes slid his arms under her knees and back, she stirred and, smiling, opened her eyes.

"Daddy, it's all right. I don't hurt anymore." Wes smiled back at his daughter. "I'm glad, honey, but you do need to see the doctor and we'll be there very soon."

"No, Daddy, I'm all right. There is nothing wrong now at all. I really feel fine. I was so sick and then you prayed and I felt hot all over, especially here"——her right hand indicated a place somewhere to the left of her navel——"and then all of the pain and sickness went away and I feel wonderful."

"I think you should go to the doctor with your parents, Sarah," John said. "Jesus has made you well, but the doctor will be able to tell you just how much Jesus has done for you tonight. The doctor will help your mother and daddy not to worry about you."

Sarah smiled back at John. "All right, then let's go. I'm tired and I want to go to bed soon." She sprang up and began to walk toward the front door.

"Mommy, will I need my coat?"

Ruth was watching her daughter with unconcealed amazement. 'There's one in the closet just inside the door. I'll get it, come on." And the Hammetsons left the room and the house, leaving the three clergymen alone with what they had just seen.

ELEVEN

♦

About ten-thirty the Hammetsons returned, in a clamor of joy and wonder, through the front door and into the living room where they were awaited. Everyone agreed that by the time they had reached the doctor the problem that had sparked the crisis had unexpectedly and entirely disappeared. The physician on call, who happened to be well acquainted with Sarah's case—having treated her in various other such crises—had expressed well-contained surprise at the results of the tests that he had conducted and had voiced a desire to undertake more tests later to analyze the surprising normality that she was manifesting. Sarah stoutly maintained she was "all right," and she was sure she was well and would remain that way. Ruth had at first questioned her daughter very closely in this regard but by this time had come to believe (probably because she so deeply wanted to) that the child was indeed right and was free of the shadow of illness that had lain across her life almost all of her years.

Wes was heard, entering the house with his two optimistic women, urging caution and restraint and hoping for some change without any conclusive assurance such a change had in fact taken place.

It was John Masters who insisted nothing be done and no decisions made until morning and the daily tests had been taken; then it would be time to decide how much insulin needed to be administered, and some indication of the extent of healing would be available. Above all, he advised, nothing should be done until the doctors had completed their tests and could say what was really safe, proper and called for. This seemed to satisfy Sarah and her mother, and gave clear relief to Wes' nagging anxiety. With that the ladies departed, leaving the men to their

44

interrupted conference and the question that was so hugely unresolved.

Wes sank into a big chair with a sigh. "Still and all, John, it was a miracle. One moment she was so deathly sick in the frightening way I have so often seen before. I knew I could look forward to hours of watching her suffer and knowing it might well be touch-and-go with her; and then in the next couple of minutes she was as well as I have seen her in years. I can't think it was anything other than a work of God; and after I burned out in the ministry I had come to think such things not only didn't happen now, but that they never had. John, I don't know what to say, except 'thank you.'"

"Please don't give me any thanks or credit. As I have been telling these guys in your absence, it was entirely the power of Christ. I am just happy I was here and open to His leading at the right time."

Wes turned suddenly to Ken Baker. "Ken, are you sure you don't remember John—not at all?"

Ken shook his head slowly. "I have never met him before tonight. I have no way of saying he was not in any classes I had at Hilltop, because there were quite a few who came in from other schools nearby for one or two classes over the three years, and I can't remember them all. But he was not in my Hilltop graduating class, and did not live in the dorm with us during those years. That much I know."

John was on his feet. "Look, Ken, I cannot dispute your sincerity, but I simply cannot account for what you have just said. Let me tell you something I remember, and see if you can make any more sense out of this situation than I can. Because I do remember you. In my three years at Hilltop we were close and good friends. It was because of me you met a young lady named Valerie DuMennier—we sat beside her at a concert one night in San Francisco—and before our days at Hilltop were past you had married her, and to the best of my own knowledge you are married to her still."

For just the briefest moment, as John spoke that name, Ken Baker's eyes misted over as if there was some power, some haunting music to it that aroused deep but undefined feelings. There was a slight and sudden drawing in of breath, a reflective pause that threatened to deepen into prolonged silence. But under the pressure of all the eyes in the room Ken Baker came back to himself and shook his head. "No—I never met Valerie DuMennier. There is something about it—but, no, I don't ever remember meeting anyone by that name. It does seem faintly familiar, somehow, as if maybe I read it in a wonderful story long ago."

"Well, Wes, what do you think?" Jim Braddock was looking at his watch and shaking his head.

"I think this is the strangest business I have ever heard of. I have always prided myself on being able to detect falsehood and fraud, and I am completely convinced John Masters is exactly what he says he is, a graduate of Hilltop Theological Seminary four years after me. I feel I owe him a very great deal after tonight, perhaps more than I am yet able to appreciate. At the same time, I am sure Ken Baker is telling us the absolute truth. He is sincere and there is no motive for him to lie. There has to be an answer, and I have about decided to see to it that we keep going until we find it. You two preachers have time to think about this question, but before we are through this venture may take some money for real expenses. That's where I can come in."

John looked from one to another. "I feel so helpless. I know who I am and what I am, but no one else seems to agree with what I know."

With one quick movement Wes was across the room and clasping his hand. "Until that question is answered to all of our satisfactions, you can rely on me for anything you need."

TWELVE

◆

And the morning was the second day.

John again emerged from sleep asking questions. *Where am I? This isn't my bedroom in the parsonage in Centerville. Jan isn't beside me. This is a motel in Denver and not a house lit by the fresh California dawn, with people awaiting the ministry God will give me this day.*

Then it all came rushing back. He did not know where Jan was, nor what had happened to her. For that matter, he did not begin to know what had happened to himself. He thought again of the beard and dirt that he had discovered disfiguring his face only yesterday morning.

This was now Wednesday morning, April 4th. The last memory he had was sometime between eleven and noon on Sunday, the 1st. Whatever had happened had taken place about sixty-seven hours ago. And only in the last twenty-two hours had he been aware of himself and struggling to make sense of the circumstances to which he had awakened. So there were some forty-five hours to account for and to understand.

How could I have gone from California to Colorado in those forty-five hours, grown a beard, become dirty and unkempt and an apparent outcast from society?

That was the first impossibility. There was simply no time available for that change to have taken place. It would require a minimum of three weeks of presumably high-test alcoholic neglect to achieve what he had seen yesterday in the mirror in the adjoining bathroom. Therefore logic demanded something be wrong with his chronology, with his remembering. In spite of appearances and the assurances of recollection, there must be a larger gap in his experience—a gap whose

47

existence had not yet become apparent but that would account for what had happened and could be filled in with some indication of why it had happened.

But where, dear God, is Jan? The present occupant of the Centerville parsonage denies any familiarity with her name. The woman who answered my own telephone number did not know even my name, and the General Minutes for the denomination on file at the headquarters of this conference in Colorado did not list me at all.

Again he faced the nightmare of thinking his memories a singular delusion, created out of whole cloth by a sick mind. His stomach knotted in anxiety at the remembrance of Ken Baker looking at him without the slightest hint of recognition, and saying with obvious sincerity, "I have never met this man before in my life."

John sat on the edge of the bed, letting the agony of these events flow unhindered over him. *But I knew Ken.*

The feelings ebbed and subsided. Everyone acknowledged he did know Ken, intimately and well. He knew his seminary. Just as surely, he would know his church and the people in it. He had known the details of the funeral yesterday, being able to recall everything—except the fact that it was to be conducted by someone else. There was an even greater mystery if he was not who he remembered being; how had he come by the knowledge he had, the ideas he had, the convictions that expressed themselves in his behavior, if they had not been formed in the smelter of his past experience?

I knew enough when confronted by the crisis with Sarah to ask for the word of God as to what I should do. I received the inner direction, and followed it with results that would soon be completely and finally shown. That child was well. She had been until last night a severe diabetic, and now she was going to be found to be completely normal. Praise God.

And yesterday, in this very room, he had to believe God had really assured him all was in His care, and it would be all right. As he relived that anguished prayer of the afternoon before, he thought he could feel the words quietly inserted again in the very center of his being. It was all right—it just had to be. Whatever the explanation might be, it existed. God was in control and it would finally be all right. Jan could be trusted to Him. His own sanity was in the care of Jesus Christ.

I just have to have faith.

Would today bring the answer? *Will I find Jan today, and be restored to my place and be able to take up again my church and my ministry?* He sank to his knees beside the bed and began to pray.

Again, it seemed to him, he could sense God's presence and love in the room. *Lord, it should be enough for me to realize Your hand is upon me and somehow Your purpose is being worked out in me. I must trust Jan and all things to You. I have to believe nothing is lost, and all will finally be made right.*

With that prayer came peace, as scripturally promised and truly beyond understanding. Banished were all the doubts and fears. The questions remained, but now he was content to leave them for the future to satisfy; and they were balanced by a confidence they would finally be answered. He turned his praying to lifting up Sarah, and the joyful assurance of God's having acted rose in him. Sarah was healed.

At length he arose and began the preparations for regaining the society of others for the day. He found himself singing and laughing in the shower.

And over and over again a unique cry of praise came to his lips and was granted transformation into sound: "Whatever's right, Lord."

THIRTEEN

◆

Jan scooped up the new book cards she had just typed and walked across to the card file of books and authors. She had just begun inserting the cards for the recent acquisitions when Grace materialized out of the stacks and stopped beside her.

"Well, Jan, what did you think?" Grace said softly.

Jan looked about. At the moment no one was there within earshot. "What did I think? About what?"

"Jerry. You two went out together for the first time last night. How did it go?"

Jan sighed. "It went very well, Grace, for a first date. We had a fine dinner, a lot of good talk, and a great time."

Grace smiled. "And—?"

"And—he then took me home. We sat in the car and talked some more, and then I said 'good night' and went in, where I got a good night's sleep—and here I am."

"Well—will you go out with him again?" Grace persisted.

"I will if he asks me," Jan replied simply.

"Did you tell him that?"

"Did I tell him what?"

Grace's face clouded over briefly with impatience. "Did you tell him you hoped he would invite you out again?"

Jan laughed. "Is it important that I should?"

"You listen to me, Jan McQueen, being maidenly and coy may work very well when both of you are teen-agers, but you have to be a bit more direct after you reach your late thirties. Jerry will want to know if he has a real chance, and it is up to you to give him a clear signal he does. Men his age are not likely to risk the game with no cigar, as it were."

"I am sure you are right, but–"

"You can count on my being right, lady. I have been through this marriage mill twice, and I know what works and what doesn't."

Whatever thoughts Jan had about that she wisely kept to herself.

Another thought struck Grace: "Jerry does have a good chance, doesn't he? I like Jerry, and I think he would be just perfect for you. You aren't going to give him the go-by without giving him a fair trial, are you?"

Jan shook her head, smiling. "No, Grace, I do like Jerry and am eager to see as much of him as he will choose to let me. It really is too early to say, but I must admit he just might be the one."

"That's better. That is what I was hoping to hear."

As Grace walked off toward the main desk, Jan stood looking after her. "Yes, Jerry might be the one," she mused. "But I have thought that too many times before to place any wagers."

At least last night there had been no dream.

♦ ♦ ♦

Breakfast was a pleasant memory.

John briskly walked the eight blocks from the motel to Jim Braddock's church in the spring brightness, consciously contrasting his feelings and experiences with those of the morning before. He reached the church several minutes before the office was due to open. Jim was not there yet so he went on, retracing his steps of the day before until he came again into the space between the buildings where he had awakened that morning—at about this time, he decided, by the sight and feeling.

The place told him nothing. The newspapers were all recent issues of *The Denver Post*. Nothing could be identified as his or as something that he had brought to this place and would not normally be found here. Old cans and bottles seemed to be as expected, and there was nothing that would indicate anything of California origin or purchase. There were no clues as to when and how he had come here. From all he could see, he might indeed have been left here by some means only moments before his awakening—but by what means, and by whom, and from where? He shook his head and laughed.

51

"Whatever's right, Lord." he said aloud.

The dirty walls echoed his words.

He again looked around, trying to kindle a feeling of familiarity with this place. He tried to awaken in himself some feeling of noticing patterns or accepting shapes, as might be expected if he had occupied this as a dwelling for any period of time.

Nothing.

No feelings, no memories. He remembered awakening here yesterday. Before that, there was nothing, no connection. Not even any memories of going to sleep here, of once entering here. It was as if he had been carried here or had first come so drugged or intoxicated he could not remember.

But he did not drink. And he was even less familiar with any other narcotic that could conceivably have created such a response. So he must theorize he had indeed been carried here. By whom?

He came out again onto the street, repeating his steps of the morning before. He could see now that those steps had been completely random and without any familiarity with the path he took. He had happened to turn down the street towards the church (*was that your leading, Lord?*) and his attempts then to recall where he was going and why were of course futile, since he had never walked in this neighborhood in his entire life. That much he was now sure was true.

He had come down here to this corner. He had seen St. Matthew's Church. He had crossed as he was doing now, to enter the building through this hall. Once again he walked down the length of the hall and entered the sanctuary. Again the custodian was at work here, replenishing the visitors' cards and making sure the pencils were sharp in each pew rack. He (*Harold, was it?*) looked up and nodded a curt greeting, obviously remembering the occasion of their meeting here yesterday morning and perhaps still not sure his first impression had not been the right one.

John stood and once again soaked up the quiet sanctity that had been deposited here by generations of faithful attendees, coming week by week to worship in these pews. It was indeed a good church, a rich place. As he had begun yesterday to be healed here, he felt today the renewal of the comfort and assurance that was his in spite of the situation. After a long moment he turned and walked back through the office and into Jim Braddock's study.

Jim had just come in and was holding a package wrapped in brown paper. Without a word he passed the package unopened to John. It was obviously a book and it had come by special overnight delivery (*How much did that cost?*) from California, from the denominational office in Sacramento. Out of the quickly torn brown paper husk emerged a new copy of the familiar *Journal of the California Conference of The United Connectional Church* for the current year. This book should contain the official summary of his life in the church up until July first of last year. He held the book tight and closed his eyes.

Yesterday they had looked him up in the *General Minutes* in the Rocky Mountain Conference office here in Denver, and had found nothing. It was of course conceivable some mistake had been made in the nationwide compilation of the Journal information of all of the conferences in that year, but it was highly unlikely. The last time he had held a copy of this book in his hands it had been a tool he routinely used to look up names, addresses, and other information about colleagues and churches, and his own service record was clearly and completely included within these pages.

John quickly opened the book to the section containing the directory of the ministers of the conference. It was but a moment until he was looking at the page where his own name and record should be in normal alphabetical order. Everything looked as he remembered it, except his name and the data pertaining to his ministry were not there. The names on the page where he should have found himself were all familiar; some more than others, but there did not seem to be anything here that was wrong or different—except for the omission of all reference to himself.

Next he turned to where the appointments to the churches were detailed, the appointments that had become effective last July first. There it was: "United Connectional Church of Centerville" with the familiar address and phone number, but the name there was "Ben Richardson" followed by the number "1" and there was a different address for the parsonage. Instead of listing the address next to the church, an address on Forestview Circle was printed.

In the Journal, as he was familiar with it, his name would have been listed here with the number "5" after it, indicating on July first he had begun his fifth year of service as pastor of that church. But in this incomprehensible situation a change had been made last year and Ben had been sent to Centerville as a new pastor.

He turned to the page that listed the recent pastoral appointments by churches and found Centerville. Again, there was no reference to him; his predecessor was there until five years ago, as his own recollection required. But then Wenlock Jolley had been appointed and had served until last June, a ministry of four years.

No hint of any ministry here by John Masters. Now he turned through the roll of the churches to those he had previously served. There was nothing to be discovered there, for he remembered this roll only went back for four years except for the complete records printed every fourth year in the historical quadrennial edition of the Journal. He would have to obtain one of those to check up on his previous appointments in the unaccountable absence of his service record.

Suddenly he realized he now held out no hope that anything about him would be found in any record.

Omnesia. He had been forgotten by them.

Somehow he had ceased to exist as far as these records were concerned. There was no logical explanation that covered all of the facts. It could not be true, but it was; and he had somehow to both make sense of and find a resolution to the situation. He shook his head and then turned to find Jim Braddock watching him thoughtfully.

"More bad news?" The tone was compassionate.

"I'm not in here; there's no record of me. It is as if I do not exist."

"Yes, I know. I was watching."

"Look, I really do not understand how this can be. You just have to believe me."

"I do, John; believe me, I do. As I say, I was watching you. That is not a new book to you. You knew just where to look, and in what pages you would find what you needed. You are very familiar with that book or one just like it. I do not doubt your honesty or your sincerity."

"Just my sanity. And you are surely not alone."

"If you are insane, you are the sanest crazy person I have ever met up with. But, just for the sake of talking, let's assume for a moment you are suffering from some kind of mental condition. What could it be?"

"Beats me. Schizophrenia?"

"Not in my book. No disorientation, no erratic behavior. Maybe some kind of hysterical conversion symptoms, but that is the only possibility, and I don't feel any sense of that."

"Why not? Let's insist I'm balmy unless proven sane."

"All right. Think back on your counseling classes in seminary. Suppose, as a result of psychic shock, you came to feel you were a pastor whose career was familiar to you. Suppose you came to believe you were this man whom you admired very much, and you began to try to live his life. And the record of that person would be there."

"OK. So I 'm really somebody else who temporarily believes I was pastor for a couple of decades in California, and all my memories are made up by my deranged mind to go along with this greatly desired identity; all because I have a pastor as a good friend and find his life safer and more acceptable than my own, whatever it normally is?"

"Yeah. You've got the picture. How does it fit?"

"It would at least make some sense of the situation and explain all the facts."

"Would it? I got the impression last night that you recognized Ken Baker."

"I did. Oh sure, he had changed but not all that much. I would have known him anywhere." His voice trailed off as he grasped the implications of his recall.

"Exactly. If you were suffering from some kind of hysterical conversion syndrome, then you would be acting out a role and talking about things that had only happened in your imagination. You would not be experiencing real feelings of recognition for real people."

"But maybe I'm a parishioner of his and he has told me a lot about his seminary experiences."

"And now cannot recognize you as anyone he has ever seen before? No, John, that doesn't work. In the past twenty-four hours, you have given all kinds of testimonies to the reality of your memories, their consistency and their accuracy. I believe you are perfectly sane and you are somehow the person you claim to be and remember being."

"But Jim, that doesn't make any sense. If I truly am who I believe myself to be, why is there no record of me? The only explanation that I can still use to account for this whole thing is the idea that I am asleep and must soon wake up from the strangest and at the same time most realistic dream I have ever had."

"Fine. If you can wake up, now is the time. Come to your senses in your bedroom in California and watch in relief while I pop like a bubble and this study and everything around you vanishes."

John smiled. "Don't you think I have tried? This is no dream. It is real, and I can't begin to cope with it. If I have not arrived at crazy, how long can I keep from getting there?"

"Long enough to check up and find out what the real answer might

be," Jim Braddock said with quiet assurance.
    Again the telephone rang.

FOURTEEN

♦

The ultimate result of the telephone call was that, just before one o'clock that afternoon, John and Jim Braddock met Wes at a fine mid-town restaurant for lunch. When the reserved booth had been occupied and the orders given, Wes turned to Jim Braddock and asked, "Is there any news?"

John interrupted, anticipating Jim's reply, "How's Sarah?"

Wes grinned. "She's just fine. Couldn't be better. She goes in tomorrow morning for a complete battery of tests, but her blood test this morning was entirely normal—very unusual, believe me. Absolutely unheard of. Ruth is convinced we all witnessed a miracle last night."

"Praise God," John responded. "That's what we like to hear."

Jim redirected the conversation: "John spent the morning with a copy of the *Journal* of his California Conference that I promoted for him yesterday. He hasn't told me yet what he discovered, but as I told you when you called, he is not listed in any place where he should be, according to his remembrance of this book."

Wes nodded thoughtfully. "That is, of course, the big difference, the puzzle. But did you find anything at all, not pertaining to yourself, different from your memories?"

John placed the book under discussion on the table before him and riffled the pages to accompany his reply. "Yes, but it took a long time before I became aware of it. I spent my time going over the daily proceedings of the four days of the conference session in Sacramento last year. At first I couldn't see anything different at all; it seemed I was reading the account of the same meeting I remembered. But then, in the minutes for Thursday afternoon I came upon this: 'Oscar Wahrheit

57

moved to amend by deleting the words, "and the roots of homophobia." Duly seconded. After some discussion the question was called, and the amendment lost.'"

"That didn't happen in the meeting where you remember taking part?"

John laughed. "I'm afraid this kind of thing doesn't keep my attention long enough for me to remember whether such an amendment was offered or what might have happened to it. No, the thing that struck me was that it was Oscar who offered it."

"Oscar dropped out of the active ministry at least ten years ago. Oh, he is still listed as a minister of the conference; but he is teaching in a junior college somewhere downstate and he simply never comes to annual conference sessions. So I immediately checked up on him. His service record is very different from what I remember it being. The last church he served in my memory was a little church in a small town at the southern end of the conference. I always thought he was left in that rather frustrating place a bit too long, and he became discouraged with his experience of ministry and turned to another field where the hours, remuneration, and satisfactions were to be preferred to the experiences that he had been having. But his service record here shows he went on serving churches until in the last couple of years he has been serving one of the best appointments in the conference.

"But that isn't the most interesting thing. I remember his ministry in that career-ending church to have extended through six years; this shows he spent only four years there, and then moved to a pleasant suburban church in the Sacramento area."

"And?" nudged Wes.

"And this, the man who had been serving that church was moved that year to the church I remember serving during all those years. Because I wasn't there, the opening occurred and Oscar was moved, saving him for the pastoral ministry."

"And do you think this was a good thing?" Jim asked.

"Yes, I do; I really do. Oscar was a fine, sound young pastor who was growing in his discovery of the things of the Spirit, along with the rest of us. I have always regretted his turning away from the local pastorate, because I felt we needed more of his kind in our churches. It was a waste and a tragedy as far as I was concerned that he went to teaching in college when he could have been doing so much in the church."

The salads were now being served, and the conversation was suspended while three hungry men addressed themselves to a succession of plates of well-prepared and much desired food. For an extended period they occupied themselves with eating and incidental comments until finally the plates were taken away and only the coffee remained. Then, once again, Wes brought them back to the subject of their meeting.

"Did you discover any other differences in that Journal, besides the one involving the pastor who continued to serve?"

"Yes I did," said John. "There seems to be another pastor missing. I have looked all through the book and found nothing about him."

FIFTEEN

◆

It was, when you thought about it, rather remarkable John should have missed Ralph's name at all; they had so little to do with each other. They had never served churches on the same district, and so only saw each other at the annual conference meetings once a year. There they spoke or sometimes only nodded greetings, but not with any great warmth. They were just not deeply involved with each other.

But there had been one occasion, some fifteen or sixteen—perhaps even seventeen—years ago when, late one evening at conference, serving on the same discussion section that was in vogue that year as part of the process of hearing reports and considering proposals for action, they had fallen into a long conversation. John could remember the after-midnight dialogue in the all-night coffee shop, the intensity that Ralph had used to detail the problems he faced in his local church, and the uproar provoked by his wife's choice and style of dress. There was indeed a good deal of feeling that had come across from Ralph on that occasion; and John had attempted to understand and accept and affirm in the best and most suitable pastoral style, just as he might have dealt with a crisis for a husband in his own church. For perhaps an hour and a half he had sat and listened to Ralph and eased himself into the stream of words from time to time to make such suggestions and remarks as seemed useful to him, in helping the other man cope with his deeply felt problems.

Now Ralph's name was nowhere to be found in the *Journal*. And the puzzle was, why not? He might have dropped out of the ministry or moved to some other conference. He could have died or become chronically ill. Any of those things might have happened. But, if the pattern that was emerging held true, Ralph's disappearance from the conference record would somehow tie in with his own. Either it arose out of some chain of events that had become different because John Masters was not included in the recipe for the entire mix; or that midnight conversation was more significant in its consequences than he had thought it to be at the time.

If only he had perfect recall. There must, in fact, be dozens of ways this Journal differed from the one that he had held in his hands as recently as a week ago. The list of appointments to the various churches must be full of little differences, if only he could remember with accuracy where everyone had been stationed. The fact he had not served in those five churches would affect whole chains of church appointments. Churches were not all on the same "level" in terms of salary, prestige, and desirability. When a "good" church fell open, it was quickly filled by someone from a church "less good," whose now empty church was in turn filled by a pastor from a still "lower" church, and so on. So it was not just a matter of who had filled the churches that he remembered serving, but rather how far-reaching the dislocation in the chains had been because he had not been involved in them.

Had the whole pattern of Ralph's life been changed because John had not been present that night to counsel him and perhaps enable him to get a handle on his problem? Looking back, he did not feel much had been accomplished in that one after-hours session. But then again, he was aware he had made some momentous decisions in his own life as the result of conversations when the one with whom he was talking could never be aware of the part he had played in John's decision for change.

As John told his two friends the details of this remembrance and what he recalled of Ralph's subsequent career, as compared with what this journal now showed, he found himself talking matter-of-factly about the differences between two worlds—the world that he had known where he had an acknowledged place and part in the lives of colleagues and churches, and this present world where somehow that participation had never taken place. He spoke of this discrepancy as an accepted reality without any pretense of being able to explain how there could be two worlds for him when everyone else experienced only one.

But he was no longer qualifying his recollections either to himself or aloud with any suggestion that they were based on any personal unreality or failing. He did not speak of them as dream or fantasy or illusion. Rather, he regarded them as inexplicable reality; and the men to whom he spoke clearly considered them the same way.

It was Wes who made this fact itself an item of discussion.

"John, I think we have gotten beyond the question of asking whether this thing has happened to you. I think the question we must now consider is just what has caused this and how? I have to tell you I googled Rev. John L. Masters this morning and am prepared to swear that you are not real. You just don't exist. Have you any insights or ideas on this score?"

"None in the world. I am open to suggestions. All I know is the last thing I recall from my world is that I was preaching in my own pulpit in my accustomed place in Centerville. I don't remember stopping or finishing or have any idea what kind of transition took place between there and my awakening here."

Wes lit his after-lunch pipe and blew out the wooden match. "It would appear to me the answer is really quite simple, on the basis of the science-fiction I have read in my lifetime. In those stories, this situation takes place all the time. You have merely been displaced by some cosmic accident into an 'alternate probability world' where, for some reason, you have never been born. Science fiction writers don't have any trouble with such situations. They postulate an infinite number of universes corresponding to each event where a choice is made. So when someone decides between going this way or that, at that same moment a new universe in yet another dimension comes into existence where the alternative that seems not chosen to us was actually taken. Then subsequent events following from that choice take place. Such heroes and villains can and do find themselves in situations that closely resemble yours."

John smiled. "Yes, I have read some of those stories too. Great entertainment. It is not truly an acceptable explanation, although of course I did consider it. But I had to reject it as having any kind of reality."

"Why must it be rejected?" asked Wes.

"Because it will not stand my scrutiny as a theologian. Science fiction writers are always talking about it being acceptable to the 'science of mathematics' when they know perfectly well mathematics is a matter of human symbols and not any kind of observational discipline at all. So we can manipulate symbols as we play games with words. If we cannot achieve the desired effect under the rules of the game as we have been playing it, then we can monkey with the rules themselves until we achieve a result or the possibility of a result that satisfies our supposed needs. But such a supposition about alternative probability worlds would mean, in a final cosmic sense, there was no reality to moral choice at all."

"But how does that follow?" Wes asked.

"Well, we would have to also postulate an infinite number of kingdoms of God to accommodate or to fail to receive each one of us on the basis of both our choosing and our failing to choose, on a number of different occasions, to follow God's will and to become the persons He is creating us to be. So long as science fiction writers are simply materialistic in their outlook, they can get away with such creative fantasies. But were they to begin to consider a reality that was theologically valid, then the shallowness of their ideas would become apparent."

"So the problem is theology?" Jim asked.

"Yes. Ultimately, such a consideration would have to fragment the world and God Himself on the basis of His creative and redemptive choices, and this then becomes patently ridiculous. Polytheism is enough of a blasphemy with respect to the usual pagan pantheons or when it emerges in the teaching of the Mormons in doctrines they themselves do not really understand. But a polytheism where reality is filled with infinite variations on the same Deity, and where He has in balance as many derivative creations where He did not act redemptively as those where He did, is simply ludicrous."

"It does complicate things" Wes agreed.

"And I cannot accommodate any ultimate purpose or meaning to a reality where there are a number of persons identifiable as myself. Could we postulate some ultimate reunion, some final drawing together into an integrated personality, where any kind of character was discernible? In fact, the whole purpose and value of choice and experience is destroyed by such a concept."

"But what if we ignore God and simply think as the scientists want us to think," suggested Jim.

"Then we find finally that the basic laws of science are totally violated by this proliferation of matter-state dimensions with no energy-source postulated for the enormous outpouring of atoms and organized energy states these new worlds would involve."

Jim laughed. "It makes a good story, but in reality it doesn't compute."

"It cannot operate in a world created by our God; and there is no possible model for it happening in a world without a very hyperactive Creator."

Wes leaned forward. "But what then is the explanation? You are real enough, and you have convinced me of the reality of what you call 'your world.' Does your world still exist and can you get back to it? We must try to discover where and how it diverged from this world as Jim and I know it, and have always known it."

For a long moment John looked down and did not reply. "I obviously have no answer to most of that question. I am convinced my world did exist. It had to. But I must also acknowledge I do not believe it exists now. I am completely at a loss to understand what has happened. My situation is that I seem to be a forty-five-year-old displaced person, with no home, no verifiable past, and a most uncertain future. My profession is gone, it would seem to me."

Jim shook his head. "You are surely a pastor, and to all appearances a good one. Why would you not be able to take up your profession again?"

"What is my professional degree; where and when and by whom was I ordained; and how do I prove it? No United Connectional bishop or cabinet is going to think highly enough of my story to trust me with one of his churches."

Wes was thoughtful. "We don't even know whether or not you might exist here in our midst, doing something else."

"And I am not in any way prepared to take up my life where I have found it and leave all of these questions unanswered. I must find my wife if she is to be found. I have got to discover the answer to your question, the most important one for me I can think of. 'Where and how does this world diverge from my own?' I feel sure, when I know the answer to that, I will begin to have the possibility of understanding what has happened to me."

Jim nodded. "I agree. That has to be the first order of business for you. I don't see how anything else is possible for you until you get to the bottom of this whole mystery."

John rubbed his cheeks with his fingers nervously. "Yes, but how do I do that? How do I eat? Where do I live? How can I do the travelling that I will need to do with no job, no money, and no real identity?"

"That is where I come in," said Wes. "As of now, you are a special employee of my firm, with your one job to find out what you can and report back to me."

"Do you mean it?" asked Reverend Jim Braddock.

"I set aside eighty thousand dollars for salary and expenses for the first year in a special account this morning before coming here. I think you can say I mean it."

SIXTEEN

◆

Easter Sunday morning, April 15th, found John Masters walking slowly up the sunlit pink cement walk, past the black enameled railing, toward the ornate main door of the United Connectional Church of Centerville, California. All around, persons familiar by sight to him (and some not so familiar) were hurrying in to fill the church for what was proclaimed on the outdoor signboard as the second of two identical services for this festive morning. John walked slowly, drinking in all of the familiarity and recognition, his whole being flooded with a joy of self-confidence mixed with the deeply painful awareness of what was lost and missing in his life.

As he turned from the sidewalk to come up the walkway to the church doors, he passed on his right the house where—*was it only two weeks ago?*—he had last seen and breakfasted with his wife, Jan. It was difficult to identify anything that was at all different. The rose-colored sidewalk, the black railings beside the steps, and the ornate doors were just as he remembered them. Familiar faces bustled past in anticipation of the coming service of worship—but familiar faces that looked at him with the intention of friendliness but without any hint of recognition. He was a stranger, being treated with conscious welcoming warmth by those to whom he could remember being friend and confidante and pastor.

He studied his former house with special care as he walked by. The front room had been transformed into a classroom, with chairs and tables and a chalkboard. Through the window he could see it was no longer the living room. Similarly he could glimpse enough in the upstairs bedroom that he had shared with his wife to ascertain it was

66

now someone's office.

When he had first been approached about becoming pastor here, the district superintendent had told him it was understood by the people that pastors were no longer willing to live in church-owned parsonages adjacent to the church, where they might be easily and continually found; and the board was willing to provide housing in one of the nearby subdivisions for their new pastoral family. John had hurriedly told his superior it was his (and Jan's) personal preference to live in the parsonage on the church grounds, and no other arrangement was needed or desired. The superintendent had expressed distinct surprise.

Obviously that conversation had turned out differently with another minister taking the role formerly assigned by providence to John. He thought back over the many times when his doorbell had been rung late at night and early in the morning. Most such callers, of course, were transients, beggars, and frequently sly indigents who knew exactly how to "work" churches and pastors for whatever they could get. For them, the fact there was no pastor on the premises would make no great difference. They would go on down the street until they came to the next church, and the next, just as they did anyway, milking Christian concern and willingness to help for every dime that could be squeezed out of those who felt themselves under Scriptural command not to judge but to be generous and loving. But there were times, too, when the needs for assistance and support were real and cruelly valid. He had only to remember his own treatment in Jim's church on that morning of his awakening to be reminded again that it was always best to err on the side of generosity and understanding.

Now he took a place in a pew in his familiar church and looked at the pulpit that had been his until two weeks ago, when whatever it was that had happened had broken off the familiar links of the chain of reality and plunged him into confusion. He glanced at his watch. It would be almost twenty minutes before the service began, plenty of time to watch and observe, and to think.

What an eventful two weeks these had been. That first Monday was and probably would be forever lost. Where he had "been" that day—if indeed he had been anywhere—was a mystery for which he could find no insights at all. On Tuesday he had awakened in Denver in clothing and uncared-for body that seemed to indicate he had lived a life of oblivion and personal neglect for at least weeks, perhaps for months or even years. The only thing that seemed to militate against a long period was the fact that while he was dirty and unkempt, he was not in bad physical health. His body was not suffering from the effects of malnutrition, or any degeneration due to dissipation. That had been the day of his remembering in the sanctuary of St. Matthew's Church and the day when he had met and convinced his new friends, Wes Hammetson, Ken Baker and Jim Braddock. It had been that evening he had prayed for Sarah.

How he praised God for Sarah's healing. For now there could be no doubt. The extensive tests had been done and then incredulously done again. The doctors had been amazed by the sudden change in this afflicted girl, who now had completely normal pancreatic function and was living a life of everyday health, instead of the predicted life of scrupulous moment-by-moment care and lurking danger.

On Wednesday he had been offered the financial help and backing of the Hammetson abundance in finding the answers to his own situation and in getting him back to some kind of normal life. Had it been merely pity or some attempt to give charity to him, he would not have agreed; but it was obvious Wes had a real and burning interest in discovering whatever answers and explanations there might be to this dilemma. Since this was the one slim ray of possibility in a world otherwise apparently unaware of his existence and uncaring about either his past or his future, he had accepted persuasion while expressing a gratitude almost as deep as he really felt.

The next several days had been occupied with several tasks. Under the guise of his "employment" by the Hammetson Insurance Brokerage Office, he had a fingerprint check run on himself by the local police department.

Now John's major problem was becoming again an officially documented "person." He absolutely required a birth certificate and was quite at a loss as to how one might be obtained. It turned out Wes had an in-law with some connection with either the N.S.A. or the C.I.A—John never inquired too closely which—and within hours Wes produced a seemingly valid birth certificate showing all of John's birth statistics as he himself remembered them. He suggested to Wes that trouble might ensue if and when someone wrote to the registrar in San Diego seeking a copy of that document, only to be told, "They have taken care of that possibility." He asked no more questions.

With this certificate in hand, he had contacted the Social Security Office requesting a social security number. No questions were asked, and the number was issued without delay.

Then the F.B.I. check on his fingerprints came back. No record. This person's prints were not on file.

They undertook to give him a realistic personal reality as far as society was concerned. Wes went with John to the local Department of Motor Vehicles office and saw him through the process of being examined and licensed to drive. They indeed needed the birth certificate, but there arose the question of whether and when he had previously been licensed. He claimed to have had his wallet stolen, and his expired, out of state license lost. John was fearful of a possible interstate computer check, but the bored clerk merely sent him to apply as a new and previously unlicensed driver. After waiting almost two hours, John was finally given the opportunity to demonstrate sufficient skill with a vehicle to be authorized to drive the public roadways of Colorado, and a few days later his all-important license arrived.

In the meantime John spent his days in the public library in Denver, going over the recent files of newspapers and news magazines, attempting to discern any differences between what he read and what he remembered. He found nothing. The event that had caused the radical dislocation of reality in his life was seemingly a private thing, not at any great distance from his own person. They had decided in long hours of discussion that the further away from his own life this *event*—whatever it was—had happened, the more lives would be touched by it. So it might well be manifested in some number of differences that he and only he would be equipped to detect. But he had found nothing.

On Sunday he had gone to St. Matthew's Church to participate as a worshipper in the Palm Sunday Service led by Jim Braddock. With the celebration of the coming of Jesus and of His self-sacrifice that would follow His triumphal entry, came also an awareness of a new birth of hope in his own life. He felt himself to be in truth the ultimate Job, having lost everything and been left discarded and alone, hearing (or thinking he heard?) the voice of God out of the whirlwind and storm, and believing that, in the Hand of such a One, all could yet be well. He had once more affirmed his submission to the will of the Loving God, and had sought to be raised to new life with Jesus Christ, a Christ Who was felt to be very near and eager to give victory and power for the doing of His will.

This week had been the time for reservations and tickets and unthinkable amounts of traveler's checks in preparation for setting out on his quest. It was agreed he would move upstream in the river of his remembrance, starting at the last place he could recall and going then, in reverse order, to the churches he had previously served. After that he would go to the seminary, his college, and finally to the places connected with his growing up and birth. He would keep his "employer" and his two pastoral friends up to date on everything he found, and they would confer by telephone daily on the significance of whatever he might turn up.

So, last night he had flown to Sacramento and had stayed overnight at the airport hotel. It was only after he arrived and checked into his lonely room that he realized this was his forty-fifth birthday, but found little to celebrate in his loneliness and desolation. Then this bright Easter morning he had rented a car and driven the familiar foothill highways to Centerville.

A movement at the other end of the next pew caught his attention and he looked up. His reverie ended abruptly, for sitting down there and opening the bulletin was a man he recognized, a man whom he knew to be dead.

SEVENTEEN

◆

On Easter Sunday, to be confronted with someone risen from the dead. . .

But there could be no question about it. The last time he had looked upon the face of George Drake was in the funeral chapel almost two years ago as he had entered and walked past the casket on his way to the podium to conduct the funeral for this fine old man. Before that, he could remember George in his original good health, the trip that he and his wife had taken, the illness that had begun in the course of that strenuous and exciting pilgrimage, and the deepening complications and failing strength that had led first to hospitalization, then through intensive care in the special unit of the hospital to final collapse and death.

But what role had he played in that chain of events, so that his removal from the life of this man had resulted in saving his life? Somehow, he had caused the death of this man by existing and coming to be his pastor. There had to be a chain of causality linking their lives together so that he had been instrumental in starting the sequence that ended in death for a man who had never done him any harm. Or perhaps this was at last evidence this "world" was different from his own, but was unrelated to him and what had happened to him. He had to find out.

On impulse he leaned toward George and whispered to him across the back of the pew. "It's good to see you looking so well, George. Have you recovered now from the effects of your trip?"

The aging eyes regarded him uncomprehendingly and without recognition. "What trip are you talking about? It's been years since my wife and I went anywhere, 'cept to Sacramento."

"I thought you and Emma went to Europe a year or so ago."

"No. We talk about it sometimes, but she's the stay-at-home kind of woman and I guess now we're both too old to start traipsin' to far places." He continued to look frankly at John as if considering whether or not to ask what right a total stranger had to address him by name and to be also aware of the name of his wife; but after a long minute, he turned back again to the bulletin and the preparation of his hymnal for the joyous service whose beginning was drawing ever nearer.

John thought back, trying to remember the circumstances of the trip that he could remember them making. It had in fact been Emma, George's wife, who had become enthused about seeing "the old country" and had persuaded her husband to undertake the five-week journey back to the English root-land where both of his parents had been born. The exact sequence of events was not clear to John because he, himself, as pastor had not really paid any attention to the trip until the Sunday School class of which the Drakes were a part had given them a "bon voyage" party one Sunday evening. He and Jan had of course been invited.

That was it. In the course of that evening Emma had said something about being inspired by a program at her women's circle some weeks before to want to go. A lady from outside the church, a minister's wife from another town, had spoken of her own trip and showed slides of what she had seen. And how had this program been obtained? John was sure now, as he thought about it, that Jan had seen or heard a sister in parsonage living at some district meeting and had invited her to come and "be the program" at the monthly meeting she and Emma regularly attended.

So, without that program Emma had not become interested in travelling back to England. The trip had never taken place and George had not been exposed to the ultimately deadly combination of exhaustion and infection. Without Jan, the program was never suggested. And of course, without his coming as pastor there would be no wonderfully lively Jan, pastor's wife, to be part of that circle. And so George was still alive.

What a shock this would be to all of the fatalists, Christian and otherwise, whom he had known. "When your time is up, then that's all she wrote." "God has written in His book the number of your days on earth, and there is nothing you or anyone else can do about it." This was a most prevalent aspect of popular theology, and was an article of faith in the belief structure of large numbers of persons.

But here before his eyes was the positive evidence that God was not involved in setting absolute times and seasons for death. It had something to do also with our own choices, and the exercise of our freedom, and the consequences of the circumstances that arose in a fallen world. So it was true, as he had always believed: God permitted what He did not necessarily intend, and God's foreknowledge of events was not in fact His prior determination of how those events would take place.

For, of course, there could be no question God knew, absolutely and precisely, all that would happen. The common assumption, indeed the necessary deduction, that human beings—time-trapped and awash in cause-and-effect relationships——made was that if God indeed had such knowledge it had to be because He had caused these events. If someone could predict the outcome of a sporting event with absolute precision, it was clear he had taken (or had knowledge of) steps to "fix" its outcome. It was almost impossible for humans to picture a reality where this was not the case.

But John had learned at least to express the verbal formulation of such a reality: God, the Creator of space and time (or space-time in the thinking of Einstein) was outside of that reality He had created. Therefore all time, from the first moment of the creation of this cosmos where we live to the last moment of its continued existence, was *now* to God. For God there was no past and no future, only a great mosaic of related present events in (at least) four dimensions rather than our standard three. God then knew everything he, John, would ever do or say; not because God had caused him to do or say it, but because He was already watching him in the choice and the act and seeing the consequences. Each human was therefore free to choose; but God had already seen the choices, and was at work bringing His purposes to fruition in the light of those choices and their relationship to His will.

That brought John back with a start to his own situation. What possible event could have produced the effects from which his life seemed to be uniquely suffering? It was not George Drake after all who was the greatest anomaly present in this room; it was rather John Masters.

And at that moment the organ swelled with the prelude; and the Easter Service, the celebration of the Rising from the Dead, began.

EIGHTEEN

♦

He couldn't help himself. The effect of the service upon him was that of having invited a guest minister to come and take his place during a temporary absence, and then finding he did not have to be gone after all, and coming at the last moment to sit in the service, incognito. Except, of course, he would never have gotten away with sitting where he was unnoticed and unrecognized in such circumstances. He kept expecting the preacher would stop and greet him, or make some reference to his being there in passing; but naturally nothing of the sort happened. He was neither ignored nor noted.

The sermon was solid and useful, straightforward and evangelical. It was obvious the bishop and the cabinet—the seven superintendents of the districts of the conference—in seeking a minister to serve this church had been careful to renew the Biblical and personal emphasis that had characterized this congregation when he himself had been appointed to it five years earlier. John knew Ben Richardson, the pastor who stood now in the familiar pulpit, by sight and by reputation, although they had never been situated close enough in the churches they served to become personal friends. His people were in good hands.

But he could not avoid the feeling that they were and would remain his people. The organist, the choir, the ushers, the people sitting around him in the pews were (with the obvious exception of George Drake.) those he would have expected this morning had he given any thought to it those impossible two weeks ago when he had been standing where Ben now stood. There were faces whose absence he noted, and there were faces that seemed to him strange and unknown. But this was the second of two services, and many of those whom he might have expected to see might well have attended the earlier service; and of course Easter was always the day when strangers and chronic non-attenders came forth to manifest a sudden and usually short-lived interest in worship participation. This was not unusual in Centerville.

And yet John felt quite sure some of the strange faces were not strange to the people sitting around him, and they represented a real divergence from the reality that he had known. His mind went back to the record that he had read in the Journal. Five years ago Wenlock Jolley had been appointed and had lasted four years. Jolley was a man of limited imagination and impact, whose appointment would have come on the basis of years of service and faithfulness, rather than suitability to a pulpit of this size and nature. Yet, of course, strange as it might seem, every pastor had his own unique following. It was an acknowledged truth, no matter how bad a preacher might be (including the legendary oaf of whom the unnamed bishop had commented, "He is supernaturally dull—no one could preach as badly as he does without Divine help.") there would nevertheless be someone who felt he was God's particular and unique gift, and there would never be another like him.

The four years, up until last July, when Jolley had occupied this pulpit might well have taken its toll of the familiar faces John could not find this morning. Several of those absent were people who had joined the church in his own pastorate, and perhaps under the altered circumstances wandered off to become affiliated with other churches. Now Ben Richardson had been here for almost a year and persons might well be attracted to Ben who would not have been drawn to hear John and to join under his own pastoral guidance.

But John had not been prepared for the experience of being in the midst of people whom he knew and loved and had served in varying intimate and acute ways, and then having the consequences and remembrances of all those hours and agonies swept away from their hearts and faces into oblivion. He found himself staring intently into the eyes of a person whose burdens he had shared and whose needs he had at least attempted to meet, hoping somehow this person would break the spell under which the world seemed to be living , cry out in recognition, and welcome him. But, of course, he or she stared back at him as one might at an incautious and brash stranger, and turned away. He sought some hint of recognition, some smile of shared friendship, but it was not there.

And the pain was constant, the loss unbearable. These people were important to him, and the relationships he had built in his five years with them was a boundless resource and treasure. Now it was gone, as his wife was gone, as his career was gone. There could no longer be any doubt of the reality of his memories. He knew this place too well and was entirely familiar with details that would be unknown to a casual visitor. He could visualize what lay hidden behind every closed door, and knew well the location of every light switch and thermostat.

So all of the "possible" explanations were finally disposed of, and he was left with the *Event* for which there was and seemingly could be no explanation. His whole life had been a dream from which all had awakened, except himself. He could only hope that, somewhere, somehow, in his personal tracing of the dimensions of this *event* there would begin to emerge some hint of what had taken place. Yet even if he could find answers, would this give him back his wife and his purpose?

He looked up at the Cross on the wall beneath the beautiful stained glass portrayal of the Risen Christ. He thought he felt the voice of God speak again in his heart with power and with peace, *Trust Me. Trust Me.*

It was surely the word he needed.

On the way out following the service, he was repeatedly greeted as a stranger and warmly invited to return.

NINETEEN

♦

Shortly after seven that evening, John again strolled up the walkway leading to the church doors. No cars seemed to be parked nearby, and so he had to wonder whether there was any possibility at all a prayer group similar to the one he met with on most Sunday evenings might be meeting in the church this Easter night. From an adjoining building came the sounds and lights of a youth group, probably very much like the one that had met there in his own experience three weeks ago.

He had spent the afternoon walking the streets of Centerville, trying to detect changes and divergences from his memory of businesses, landmarks, and the people who left signs of themselves in lettered doors or the tasteful outdoor signs permitted by a conservative city government. He had found nothing. He could not find a single certain difference in what he saw from what he expected to see. There were some things that did surprise him, but he could not be sure he was not merely seeing more because he was looking more carefully; Jan would know. She was much more observant than he was. How often he had brought home the news of some business change only to be informed this had taken place some time before, and he was tardy in noticing what his wife had long since seen and accepted.

He was quite sure he would find no one at the church tonight. He himself had started this Sunday Evening Prayer Service, and it had never grown large. At most, it had included a dozen or fourteen people, and often it numbered but five or six. Still, it was a source of strength and grace and had been the instrument for some great works of God. Frankly, he felt he needed to meet with such a group tonight, although what he would say to them and how he would share with them any hint of his predicament was beyond his imagining.

The door was open, but the church was dimly lit and quiet as he went in. No one was in the sanctuary, but they usually met in the Ladies' Parlor anyway, so he went there. He turned on the lights, and sat down to await anyone who might come. Idly, he picked up a Bible from a nearby table and looked at the cover. "Given in Loving Memory of Mary C. Talbott." He felt sure this same Bible had been in this room when he was last here. He opened the pages and began to read.

It must have been several minutes later that he became aware of a figure standing in the doorway. "Can I help you, Mister?" It was Carl Heinrich, the church custodian. John looked up and then remembered he must not assume a familiarity he felt to be appropriate but would not be in keeping with Carl's experience of him.

"Ah, no. I was hoping there might be a prayer group meeting in this church tonight, but so far I seem to be out of luck."

"As far as I know, nobody will be meeting. At least, they haven't told me."

"Is it all right if I am my own group for a few minutes? Will I be keeping you from something by being here?"

"Oh no, stay as long as you like. I saw the light and came over to see what was happening, but I won't lock up for another hour or so." Carl turned and disappeared through the door.

John looked back to the passage he had been reading, but he couldn't get himself again into it. No one was coming. He might just as well go out and get in the car and head back for Sacramento. He laid the Bible down.

Wait.

What? What was that?

Wait.

That one word spoken in the depths of his being was enough. John bowed his head on his hands and began to pray. With prayer came a sense of peace, of submission, of trusting, and of that confident expectation that is called "hope." For some minutes he thus remained. All was quiet. Nothing stirred.

Then there was the unmistakable sound of the front door of the church opening and closing quietly.

For the brief spell of perhaps ten seconds John forgot the events of the past fortnight. Someone had come into the church and it was his privilege and responsibility as Pastor to see if there was something that he could do for them.

He got up and moved quickly through the door, down the short hallway and into the back of the quiet sanctuary. Halfway down the aisle a woman was standing, silhouetted against the light that illuminated the Christ window and the altar, making the window visible to passersby outside. She was standing looking at the altar and the cross as if undecided what to do next. Upon hearing the sound of his shoes on the carpet she turned abruptly toward him.

"Are you the minister?"

This was indeed a question. He had surely been appointed to this church at the last Annual Conference he had attended and the circumstances of his removal were at least questionable at this moment. Besides, there was no other minister available here at this time of night.

"May I help you?"

The light illuminated a young face, overcast with anxiety. "It is my husband—he is at the hospital. We were camping and he became ill—and I brought him in to emergency, and now he is in intensive care, and I am so afraid." With that she began to sob.

John laid his hand gently on her shoulder. "What does the doctor say? What is wrong?"

"He says, 'cerebral aneurysm'—something like a stroke, but even more dangerous."

In his mind's eye John pictured the weakened spot in the blood vessel, the swelling bubble as it gave out, and the calamitous bursting into the vulnerable surrounding brain tissue. "Your husband is not conscious?"

"No. I had a terrible time dragging him into the car. I really don't know how I did it. I was afraid he would die right there."

"But you made it. You got him to where he can be helped."

"Yes, but the doctor does not give me much hope. He says he doubts whether Ralph will ever regain consciousness. It is so hard." Once again, tears.

John was listening now to two voices. The one spoke of fear and doubt and grief; the other, the one within, was speaking of strength and power and victory.

"Let's go back to the hospital together. Would you like me to pray for Ralph?"

"Yes—oh, yes. Please come and pray. Anything. Please."

"Is your car here?"

She had to look at him for a moment before she could answer. "No, I left it in the parking lot at the hospital. I just had to walk, to get away and think. I don't know why I ended up here."

John smiled to himself. He knew. Just as he knew why he had come here tonight and why he had been told to wait. "My car is out front. Come on, let's go."

He took her arm and guided her down the steps and out to the curb where his rental car was waiting. They climbed in and drove the few blocks to the local hospital.

As they hurried down the long hallway toward the closed door marking the boundary of the intensive care unit, John spoke softly. "What is your last name?"

"What?"

"What is your last name? I am asking to see Ralph who?"

"Oh. Polanski. Ralph Polanski. He is in bed D."

They stood together while John rang the bell summoning the supervising duty nurse. After several minutes she appeared.

Again John had that eerie experience of being unrecognized by a face well known and familiar to himself. "I would like to come in and pray for Ralph Polanski. I am his pastor."

He knew what was going on in the nurse's mind. The slight flicker of surprise in her eyes came with the thought that somehow a pastor had come so quickly from Polanski's home church, however far away that might be. At the same time, Ralph's wife might notice the fact he called himself their pastor, rather than the local pastor of their denominational church that she had turned to in her need. The ambiguity of exactly who he was and where he came from was necessary under the unique circumstances. But the nurse glanced at the wife and the Bible and opened the door to admit them.

With but a few steps they were within the cubicle and beside the bed where a young man lay unconscious. He was wired to a monitor for his vital signs, and various tubes conveyed nourishment and medication into his veins. Young, good looking, pale.

I am here, Lord. What would you have me do?

Clearly, the directions came. John reached out and gently laid his hand upon the forehead of the unconscious man. Within himself, the prayer he began consisted only of the praise of The Father and of Jesus Christ. He felt the inner joy leap upward, the certainty of love and power rising in the center of his being. Words formed in English and rushed to his lips for expression.

"In the Name of Jesus. Thank you, Lord. Heal now, O Lord. Make new every cell, every part. Thank you, Lord. Remove all damage, create all health and wholeness. Restore now we pray, Lord Jesus, what you created first in your Word before the beginning of the world and caused to be formed and made in the womb of his mother. Thank you Jesus."

The affirmation of the Spirit within was almost too great for him to contain. It seemed to John as if the whole universe was crying out a rich *Yes* to his prayer.

And the one who was Ralph stirred.

A slight groan.

The eyelids moved faintly.

The right hand moved. Then the eyes opened and looked around, first at John and then at the young wife.

"Hi, Hon" the lips whispered. "What happened? Where am I?"

The nurse came quickly at the sound of joyful tears and stayed, transfixed by the unthinkable experience of the return to consciousness of her newest and least hopeful patient.

That first Easter could hardly have created greater surprise than this return caused in her.

TWENTY

◆

John walked slowly down the white corridor toward the front door and his car.

He had stayed long enough to savor the amazement of the doctor, who had flatly declared the return to consciousness and the apparent complete lack of brain damage as "a miracle." According to all of the tests and to his own certain knowledge, such a recovery as had taken place this night was completely impossible. Yet it had happened and the doctor was as delighted as the wife of his patient. John had remained with her outside while new tests were performed, and the doctor had come out to say her husband would be kept overnight for observation and rest after the shock he had sustained, but there was no clinical reason why he should not be released before mid-morning the next day. The last smiling words the doctor uttered were, "I cannot imagine what happened, but we should be grateful it did."

No one had linked John's presence with the event. As far as the staff was concerned, the presence of a clergyman was simply the occasion of discovering the change in the medical situation of the patient. The doctor had smiled at him and acknowledged his presence, but obviously regarded him as being unnecessary in appraising the situation as it had shown itself to be developing.

John knew this night and everything in it had been in the hands of God. He had come back for his own reasons, but God had a deeper and more important purpose for him, and by God's grace he had been open to it and had let himself be guided. Here was the joy. This was indeed what it meant to truly be alive. To see the power of God at work in the lives of others and to know God had been gracious enough to use you as the channel, the tool of His own greater love.

Thank you, Lord.

Well done, my good and faithful servant.

At any moment the nurse and Mrs. Polanski might come to compare notes on his identity and begin to wonder who he was and where he had come from. Perhaps Ben Richardson was still too new in the community to be recognized at sight by this busy nurse. She had, of course, known Reverend John Masters after five years of all too frequent encounters, at least before the *Event* that had so completely transformed all things for him.

Suppose the young lady had not found him in the church tonight and had persisted until she had taken her need to Ben Richardson; what would he have done? What would have happened? There was no clear answer to that. As far as he knew, Ben was not involved in the idea and practice of Christian healing. Not all pastors were. Ben would have been solicitous and willing to give spiritual comfort and prayer, but it was not at all certain this healing would have taken place. Perhaps it was doubtful that it would have. He himself was present and open and willing, and God had blessed him.

He thought about Wes Hammetson and the two clergy colleagues back in Denver. What would they say when he told them of the night's events? Wes seemed to think this was commonplace stuff to him, and probably would say this was "what he expected." The miraculous healing of Sarah had established in Wes' mind the simple identification of John as possessing "a gift of healing from God" that he seemed to assume meant he could effect whatever healing was needed whenever he chose to perform it. Wes seemed to think such things were a routine part of John's life. Ken Baker would still be skeptical about the whole thing, and Jim Braddock would be clearly envious.

But John could remember standing beside other patients in very similar situations and praying without the dramatic and wonderful answer he had been privileged to witness tonight. He knew the feelings that went with praying, and praying again, and persisting in prayer, while nothing visible happened. He was sure, or thought he was sure, all prayer was used by God for His good purposes; but so often prayer strengthened the soul and gave direction to the spirit without having any material effect that could be discerned upon the body. This kind of healing was special. And it was not that he had done something different to influence God; the difference had its origin in the love of

God and in the activity of the Holy Spirit. There were some times when he had come by his own choice to a bedside to pray, only to be met there by the love of Christ and to experience the joy of wonderfully answered prayer; but this time God had held him and sent him and kept him in His leading, every step of the way.

He climbed into his car, started it, and set it in motion. It was time, he thought, to get out of town. Circumstances might conspire to raise the question of whether he had this night "impersonated a pastor" if he stayed around any longer. His disappearance, on the other hand, would be a mystery that would hurt no one and might give cause to some folks to do some thinking about their faith. Besides, he wanted to move backward in the chronology of his own life and his schedule called for him tomorrow afternoon to be in Henley, the church and community he had served before coming to Centerville.

But as he drove out of town he felt yet again the full weight of the loss that he had so inexplicably sustained.

TWENTY-ONE

◆

Two o'clock the next afternoon found John driving into the town of Henley, some thirty miles south of Fresno and somewhat to the East. It lay in the fertile valley just at the foot of the hills that would swell to become the Sierra Nevada Mountains. It was a small city, now spreading to possibly ten thousand inhabitants that had grown up around the needs of the many farmers who had begun to prosper here in the final decades of the nineteenth century. Everything still hinged on the prosperity of those farmers, and the fields and orchards and vineyards formed a living tapestry into which this jewel of a city, with its buildings and modern services, was set. The road leading into town simply left behind the rows and rows of well-tended vines and trees, from which America and the world would be furnished wine, raisins, and fruit, and abruptly began to run instead through unfinished subdivisions, and then the teeming neighborhoods of totally occupied slightly older homes, finally coming into the quiet streets of houses dating back a half century or more and the central business district.

John saw much change, but he had expected this. It was now five years since he had lived here in his own experience, and changes multiply naturally in such a time. But the familiarity that should have come from nine years of serving here as pastor was flooding his awareness. If there had ever been any suspicion he was suffering from some hallucination regarding having actually lived and served here, the knowledge that he found in himself of what he would see at each corner and at every turn dispelled it. He counted back. He had been appointed to Centerville for five years. Previous to that, he had been in Henley beginning sometime in late June, fourteen years ago.

Turning at a familiar landmark he found himself approaching the church. In the yard next door children were playing. If this was still the parsonage, those children would include at least some child or children of the present pastor. His own memory was that his successor here had been an older couple whose children were grown and gone and had children of their own. He stopped the car and looked at the children and their playing again. No, he would bet they were the children of the home and not visitors. The yard looked well-used and turned over to the affairs of regular young dwellers. Chalk up another change.

There had been no children there when he and Jan had lived in that house. Not that they had not wanted children and tried for them, but somehow it never happened. The doctors could find nothing wrong in either of them, but conception simply never took place. It had been an abiding disappointment to them both.

Suddenly he found himself thinking what a good thing this was, under the circumstances. How bitter the situation would be if he had not only lost his whole career, his friends, everything he had ever done, but also had experienced the loss of his children as well. It was bad enough to have lost Jan...

Was Jan alive and well? If she was another of those who have never met or known of John Lewis Masters then surely she would be married to someone else.

John eased his car into the curb, laid his head on the wheel, and let himself cry. All of the other changes that he had experienced in the past two weeks were frustrating and overwhelming in their confusion, but the loss of his wife was pure deep pain.

The sound of his sobbing died as the storm of feeling passed and the need faded. Deep within he thought he could feel the one word he most needed.

Trust.

Yes, Lord.

Again: *Trust.*

He wiped away the tears, and put the car in motion again. He drove on several blocks and passed the high school where Jan had so often served, on call, as a substitute teacher during those nine years; and where he himself had spoken and sometimes counseled in crises of behavior or event at the request of family or administration. He thought for a moment of stopping to see his various friends on the faculty who knew him as former pastor and colleague and associate and good comrade; but he realized with a start this would only expose him once again to that blank encounter of unknowing that was accorded the brash stranger. By now there could be no doubt he would be totally unremembered by the persons he held in the greatest affection and dearest memories.

What would he prove by coming back to Henley? He had wanted to be sure the memories that he seemed to have were actual and reliable. There might have been some other explanation about his recalled experiences in Centerville, however improbable and far-fetched. But to have detailed and accurate memories also of this thoroughly disparate farm town some two hundred miles away should settle the matter once and for all.

He could not expect to have the kind of accurate awareness of the changes that the *Event* in his life had wrought in the fabric of this part of reality. Too many changes would have been noticed had he returned a month ago. But there would perhaps be some events that he might add to his catalogue of those things that had happened differently here than in the world as he remembered it and where he had a vital and integral part.

With this in mind, he checked into the one motel in town, and having settled his few belongings in the plastic room he had been assigned, he set out on foot to walk downtown. The mid-afternoon sun was warm and pleasant, lacking the intense heat that it would acquire in another few weeks. The air was heavy with the scents of blooms and blossoms. John breathed deeply. One of the reasons he had left this church was that he had been troubled all his life with mild asthma, and the spring pollens here had caused him increasing discomfort. Ordinarily a visit here at this time of year and on a day such as this would cause his lungs to become congested within minutes, and he had no doctor-prescribed drug he might take. But he could detect no sign of anything amiss in his breathing. Perhaps one of the side effects of the mysterious event he had passed through was that it cured the incurable, and his affliction had been eliminated. It was certainly a delight to be able to walk this way and in this degree of comfort along these familiar streets.

The sidewalk slid swiftly under his advancing feet until he came to the central business district. John turned at the main corner, crossed over the street and entered the battered front door of the area's twice-weekly newspaper, *The Guardian*. Everyone in that office he knew by sight, and many of them were members of his former church and friends of his since his coming to Henley almost fourteen years ago. After a glance they all went back to their various preoccupations except Jimmy Mendoza, who was obviously in charge of the counter this afternoon.

"May I help you?"

John decided abruptly on an experiment. "Yes, Jimmy. I'm doing some research work on this town and especially the United Connectional Church in the recent past, and I wondered if I might examine the back issues of your paper over the past, say, fourteen years?"

John's casual use of his name had caused a reaction, not only from the man himself, but from those nearby. They looked up in sudden reappraisal of someone who had walked in from outside unrecognized, but who could call one of them by name. Jimmy himself was obviously scouring his memory for some clue as to how and when he had met the man confronting him across the counter.

"Excuse me, Sir. Have we met?"

"Oh, yes we have. But it was five years ago or more. I'm not surprised you don't remember." John passed the matter off with a shrug.

Jimmy likewise shook his head and passed off his total lack of recall. "Sure. All of our papers six months or older are on microfilm in that room. I'll get you started and show you how to run the machine, and you can work there as long as you want." He led the way across the desk-crowded room to the designated door.

As he passed the editor at work at his cluttered desk John could not resist the temptation: "Keep up the good work, Howard——there may be another pullet surprise in it for you."

Some years before the paper had run an extensive series of articles on the modern techniques and problems of egg ranching, and the Sierra Poultry Institute had responded by awarding a special recognition to the paper, an award that some member of the staff had referred to in print as Howard's "Pullet Surprise."

How many remembered after all these years?

It was obvious Howard remembered. He half rose in his chair and stared after the departing stranger, clearly taken aback by this unexpected recognition and recall.

At the door John glanced back, saw what he had wrought, and grinned. What a story there was in this whole situation for a newspaper that could make sense out of it and convince its readers it was telling the truth. So far John had almost succeeded in convincing himself. There were also some half-convinced new friends in Denver who had given him the great gift of their trust and support.

But he needed a great deal more information and detail before any true explanation would be possible, if one ever was. That information was now to be sought in the pages of old San Joaquin Valley newspapers.

He listened while Jimmy explained to him the workings of the fiches and the reader, and then he began with the editions of the week when he could remember coming for the first time to the community.

Nine years of newspapers would require a lot of reading.

TWENTY-TWO

◆

As he read the decade-old newspapers on the screen in front of him, he began to organize the differences he sought into three categories:

First of all (and most plentiful) would be the differences in what happened in the church and its immediate and active membership, compared with his own recollection of those persons and what he could remember them doing and experiencing during those years.

Secondly, would be differences referred to outside of the church fellowship in the larger community, presumably as the result of some chain of causation that would stretch back finally to his own actions (or rather, on these pages, his lack of actions.)

And finally, he would be seeking to be aware of any event beyond Henley and its environs that might be derived from the *Event* that he postulated as having happened to cause the dislocation of his life.

The first category was too great to begin to chronicle; instead of his own nine-year pastorate the church had been served by three pastors during that period. The longest tenure had been a five year stint by Werner McKesson, appointed eleven years ago. Werner had obviously done well and been greatly loved and appreciated here, and he had gone on to a major career advancement at the conference session ending his final year.

Beyond the necessary differences in pastoral leadership was the multitude of changes in the personal lives of the members. It would have been gratifying, perhaps, if all of these changes judged newsworthy by this local Tuesday and Thursday publication had been less positive as shown than as remembered, suggesting his own presence had been a uniformly beneficial and redemptive influence; but such was not always the case. There were intimations of marital breakup and divorce that indeed had not happened in his own experience here; but there were also some sunderings he clearly remembered that had not taken place in the Henley reflected by these pages. It was especially obvious there were some members who had benefitted from Werner's work here that had not similarly been helped and inspired and empowered by his own. He had always known such was the case in theory, but it was a bit difficult to sit and examine the evidence of specific instances in black and white.

The second category of differences noted, the one caused by the spreading rings into the broader community of ripples from his presence or absence was harder to detect and identify. In a paper from the summer twelve years ago was a report of the suicide of a young female high school student he knew had not taken place in his own experience, as he had been pressed into service a year or so later as vocal soloist at her wedding in a nearby church.

The Event puzzled him for he could not reconstruct any chain of circumstances in his own mind that could connect himself or his wife with that young life in such a way as to make a difference in her thinking and acting about herself. He realized he would not be aware of everything that was accomplished in and through the lives that he touched. In this case he could come up with no solution.

In the final category he could find only one item that jarred with his remembrance of the world as it had been. It was a filler on the bottom of a column in January, six years ago:

> ### I.R.A. VISITS HENLEY
> *Calculations have shown the I.R.A. passed directly over Henley and the Alta District heading west in December, eleven years ago. It was at that time undetected, and no Camerapox was noticed locally.*

He hardly noticed it as he scanned the page and only the strange reference to "Camerapox" caused his mind to linger and then to return and read the whole item more thoughtfully. It was obvious this was a reference to something needing no elaboration in the mind of the average reader, but it left him completely in the dark. The headline suggested to him a travelling troupe of belligerent Irishmen, but clearly the initials had nothing to do with the desires of some Celts to exercise self-rule. It was some kind of phenomenon that the readers at the time would have recognized, but that he could not find in any part of his own remembrance. Whatever it was that had happened (and it had at the time been undetected) it had taken place three years before his arrival. "Camerapox" sounded like some kind of disease that attacked either cameras or film and again the term was well-enough known at the time to require no explanation in casual publication.

He was thus driven to the conclusion that for the first time he had found an event in this world that had not taken place in his own remembered life. If he could assume the only differences that he would ultimately find were in some way related to his own situation—and this was the hypothesis that governed his whole quest—then he now had his first clue to what he was looking for.

I.R.A. The letters refused to give any idea of what they might represent. But now he had a specific question to investigate.

He arose and turned off the equipment he had been using. It would be necessary for Jimmy to put everything away. He turned and strode through the door. The office outside was empty, except for one woman ad clerk at work at her desk. John paused at the door. "Thank you very much for your help and Laura, say hello to Tom for me."

Smiling, he walked out the door knowing his exit was followed by eyes puzzled by his unexpected personal knowledge.

Three doors down, he turned on impulse into the photographer's studio he had also known quite well. The photographer's wife was, as usual, working at the desk just behind the frame-filled counter. He assumed his role of stranger rather than the natural one suggested by his remembered associations and long friendship: "Pardon me, but I need to ask a question. Could you tell me about 'Camerapox'?"

She looked at him as if such a question was the last thing in the world she had expected to be asked, and then said, "I think you'd best talk to my husband about that. I'm not sure I remember enough about it." She disappeared through a curtained doorway.

After a few moments the curtains parted to admit the remembered figure of Saul Martin, source of all knowledge about things photographic. He thrust his hand forward unselfconsciously in greeting. "Hi. I'm Saul Martin. What can I do for you?"

He gripped the hand warmly. "John Masters. I thought you might explain to me this business about 'Camerapox' and the I.R.A."

Saul grinned. "I sure wish I could. If I knew what it was all about I could write my own ticket. The folks at Eastman would give a lot to know what it was that happened and what the chances are of its happening again."

"But what was it?"

"Nobody knows. For most folks, it was the strangest thing the scientists ever came up with, a real and mysterious U.F.O."

"U.F.O.—Unidentified Flying Object?"

"Yeah, only I would have called it a 'U.S.O.' —an unidentified stalling object, because it moved so slowly. They calculated it moved something like an eighth of an inch a second."

"That is pretty slow for something in flight."

"Pretty slow? About 32 feet an hour. Nothing goes that slowly, not even a balloon. The darn thing was first detected about ten years ago over the coast west of here."

"What did it look like?"

"It didn't look like anything. Nobody ever saw it. That's why it was called the I.R.A. 'Invisible Radiating Anomaly' was the term the scientists applied to it. I took my astronomical telescope—I have a good six-incher I made myself—and made the trip over at the time. Anyway I got the latest fix on it and set my scope up and must have looked right at it, but I didn't see anything. That was the problem. There was just nothing to see."

"How did they know there was anything there?"

"The thing was radiating radio frequencies, some ultraviolet, and a lot of X-rays. That's what caused all the trouble before they figured out what was going on. People's film started developing spots. 'Camerapox' it was called. Film would develop blotches when it was developed. Different emulsion batches, but the same effect—all right along a straight pathway across the country. It was a lot worse at first; real bad forty years ago, back east. Lots of pictures ruined. No explanation. Didn't affect all of any batch, just films that had been in certain areas at certain times. Didn't hardly affect us at all. Oh, I remember having a little trouble maybe seventeen or eighteen years ago, but nothing I couldn't retouch. Color slides where the worst, and they weren't too bad, you know. Like cheap processing in a careless lab. Most folks couldn't notice the difference. Later on, they traced the problem to places under the trajectory of the I.R.A. and figured it had been doing this all along its pathway for almost seventy years."

"Where is it now? What has happened to it?"

"That's the funniest thing of all. I was just reading the latest *TIME* when my wife came back to get me. Seems the thing has just disappeared. It's gone."

"They've lost it?"

"No, not that. As I said, it radiated some radio waves as well as the harder stuff, and they could always locate it after they had once discovered it and knew what they were looking for, by using radio direction-finders on its special frequency. Then, a couple of weeks ago, it disappeared. No sign of it at all."

"What do they think happened?"

"Well, they are pretty sure it was getting higher and higher as it went along, and they figure it just left the atmosphere altogether. No better explanation of its ending than they ever had for where it came from, or what it was."

A giant question formed in John's mind. "Just when did this thing stop radiating and disappear?"

"Let me go get the article and take a look. I'm sure it said."

He disappeared through the curtain, to reappear after just a few breaths. He was leafing through the familiar-looking format. "Yes— here it is.'1958 hours GMT'— that would be, let me see. . ."

"Two minutes before noon Pacific Time, two weeks ago last Sunday," John said slowly.

TWENTY-THREE

◆

TIME's coverage was upbeat and familiar without being as informative as John's interest demanded. *NEWSWEEK* was similarly offhand. A mysterious phenomenon well known to all of their readers as the result of observations and exhaustive discussions across the years had suddenly disappeared. A sketch of the history of the object was given: how it first made its presence known in New York State sometime in the late 1920's through the localized fogging of photographic film; how this strange effect decreased in area coverage and intensity over the years, all the while moving west, until it faded into insignificance and was all but forgotten. But then, ten years ago, a group in the field studying background radiation in the Coast range of California had detected a strong source of x-ray and ultraviolet radiation almost directly overhead. At first they had thought it to be some remote but very powerful supernova elsewhere in the galaxy, but they had calculated it was actually only a few miles above the earth, moving incredibly slowly in a westerly direction. Nothing was visible to optical or radar examination, but the object was obviously a "vortex of intense disturbance." Once its trajectory had been plotted, computer projections linked it up with the "Camerapox" pathway of a half century before. Scientists had continued to probe and speculate and to titillate the public with their conjectures about the object until April 1st, when it had suddenly and inexplicably ceased to radiate on any of the energy bands that had previously been excited and had seemingly disappeared.

John had quickly hurried to the library and hunkered down beside the back issues of the *SCIENTIFIC AMERICAN*, but when he interpreted the rather more ponderous nomenclature used to describe the *Invisible Radiating Anomaly* it was obvious little more was known than the news magazines he had purchased covered in their background for the disappearance.

The most interesting note came in a discussion of the fact that the object appeared to be gaining altitude as it passed further and further west. At first this had been passed off as inaccurate altitude determination, but the refinement of locating techniques and observations over a longer period of time definitely established it was slowly spiraling out as it proceeded on its labored trajectory. The greatest problem for physicists seemed to be the very slow velocity the object maintained; that, and its total invisibility.

John was finally tactfully ejected from the closing library, and he made his way back to his motel room. He threw his purchased magazines and his notebook on the bed and lay down beside them, staring at the ceiling. It was clear everyone knew about the I.R.A. He had taken time at the library to ask some of the patrons their opinion of it, and they knew what he was talking about even though many of them did not know the latest news about the object's disappearance. It was a matter of common knowledge.

To everyone but me.

He had never heard of it before that filler in *THE GUARDIAN*. He was an avid reader and always hungry for the latest information about science and technology. He was thus sure this invisible intruder had not been a part of his world, the world where he had lived before Passion Sunday. And it was on that Sunday at about the moment of his last memory as pastor in Centerville the thing had disappeared. Could this be a coincidence? It seemed unlikely. He was sure in his own mind there was a direct tie-up between this thing, whatever it was, and what had happened to him.

Or was its disappearance caused by the same thing that had happened to him? Perhaps it collided with something, destructively encountering the thing that would also have its devastating effect upon his life and peace and future. Maybe this thing exploded over the Pacific, somehow thrusting him into—personal obliteration. Alternate probability worlds were foolishness. This was the same world, the one world that existed. And yet the changes were abundant, even to his haphazard remembering. But, so far as he could determine, all of the changes pertained to him or could be related to him, directly or indirectly. At least nothing that he had seen ruled this supposition out.

This object must be related directly to him in some way. In this world it had soared out of the past, first of all in a pathway of photographic blight and then finally as an object (or at least a moving locus) that had at last been isolated and detected.

He had quite a lot of data that he had noted in his leafing through the magazine's back issues in the library. Things like dates and towns where the "Camerapox" had been noted. Not a complete record by any means, but sufficient instances to perhaps construct some kind of approximate path. Would it help to find out where it had started?

With sudden determination he bounded from the bed and made his way outside to his car. Unlocking the door, he opened the glove compartment and drew out the packet of maps he had purchased in Denver before boarding the airliner at the start of his pilgrimage. Sure enough, in the midst of the local road maps that he had expected to need was the map the airline had furnished in the seat pouch for all its passengers so they might notice the many nationwide routes they served with pride. He did not know what had made him decide to add that national map to the bundle of local ones he was carrying, but he was glad now he had.

Coming back into the room, he spread the map out on the floor and began to look for place names. There was Henley, seventeen years ago. Here was the place ten years ago where the object crossed the coast. Thirty-one years ago, Camerapox was detected in La Junta, Colorado. Forty-five years ago the I.R.A. had been passing over southern Illinois, with Sandusky, Ohio, reporting an outbreak of what was known as Camerapox sixty-one years ago. Carefully he connected the points that he had made on the map, extending the slight curve beyond the places where the first reports were made.

He looked at the name under the beginning of his line, and then looked again. Ridgeham, New York, according to his rough projections, would have been the place where this thing started out if it had indeed begun sixty-five years ago.

And Ridgeham was the birthplace and home town of his own father.

TWENTY-FOUR

◆

Jan said, "Good night, Jerry" and thoughtfully replaced the telephone on its base, breaking the connection. She leaned back on the couch.

So Jerry wanted to take her out tomorrow night, first to supper and then to a concert at the Pavilion. She had thought perhaps he had decided against continuing to date her. He had not called to ask her out since that first time; how long ago was that? Now, just as she was about to get ready for bed, he had called again—calm, pleasant, personable—asking her out tomorrow night for just the sort of evening she knew she would thoroughly enjoy.

And she had said "yes." Why not? He had explained he had not called before because he had been away on business. Where was it he said he had been? Yes, of course—he said he had been in Japan to make a presentation at some conference. No matter, he was back now and had called and asked her out, and tomorrow evening she could test her feelings about him and about what he might possibly come to mean to her.

She got up and walked toward her bedroom, pausing only to turn out the lights in the living room. Standing beside her bed, she quickly undressed, hanging up her skirt, and consigning her blouse to the laundry hamper, along with her bra, panties and pantyhose. She drew on her nightgown, slipped her feet into her slippers, and headed for the bathroom.

Within a few minutes she returned, laid back the covers on the bed, and slipped between the cool sheets. She reached over and turned out the light. Before long she was asleep.

She seemed to be in an immense, sprawling, complicated building, consisting of a maze of long, intersecting hallways in brown paneled woodwork. As things began, she had just stepped out of a room near the end of one of these hallways and was looking down its poorly lighted dark mahogany length. It seemed to her as if it were several blocks long, and she could see places on each side where other hallways intersected it. Along both sides of the hallway were doors, like the one out of which she had just come. Perhaps there were many people occupying these rooms, but no one was visible or audible. The whole place seemed silent and empty, and she felt alone.

"I am always alone," she thought. "Where should I go?"

As if from a great distance, she heard a voice call her name: "Jan."

A familiar voice, *his* voice. Somewhere in this maze, *he* was looking for her. She was about to cry out to tell *him* where she was, when she suddenly realized she was standing there entirely naked. She wanted *him* to find her, but not completely bare. What should she do? The room she had come out of must be her room, and so it must have her clothes in it. What in the world had induced her to come out into this hallway without anything on? She would go back in and get some covering, and then come out and call to *him*.

But suppose, while she was inside, *he* should come quickly and pass by and they should miss each other? Shouldn't she call out to *him* first, and then go in and find something to put on? She raised her voice, and cried, "I am here. I am here." Then she turned to hurry back to her room. But she seemed now to have come down the hallway some distance from where she had started, and she did not know which door was hers.

She would just have to try each door as she came to it—but, suppose she opened a door and went into a room and it was occupied? Suppose she went in her present state into the private room of some strange man?

She scrutinized the doors, seeking some clue that would tell her to whom they belonged. She now noticed they had large brightly polished brass oriental graphics in the center of each door, and she thought she recognized them as Japanese characters. Was she then in Japan?

Jerry was connected with Japan. Perhaps Jerry was in one of these rooms, and she would walk in on him. She really did not want to find Jerry, and she certainly did not want him to find her as she was, stark naked. She began trying each doorknob as stealthily as she could manage. None of them seemed to be unlocked.

Again she heard, "Jan." It was louder, closer.

She thought, "If *he* comes down the hall before I can find my room and get dressed, I will try to hide in the doorway. I will squeeze in as close to the wall and the doorjamb as I can, make myself inconspicuous as possible, and maybe *he* will not notice me. I am so afraid—"

She hurried on to the last door on her right. This was her door. She knew it was. It alone did not seem to have a Japanese character upon it. She tried to turn the knob. It would not turn. It was locked. Had she locked it as she came out? The key must be in the pocket of her dress, inside. Why had she ever come out without it?

Again, much closer: "Jan." *He* was coming, *he* would soon be here.

"But why am I afraid?" she said aloud. "I have stood before *him* naked before. I can remember that. *He* has seen me this way more than once." She turned and stood with her back against the door, awaiting his arrival.

But when had *he* and she been in this circumstance before? Sometimes, when she had dreamt of *him*.

"I must be dreaming now," she suddenly decided.

With that she awoke.

She lay there in the dark, reliving the now vanished vividness.

"Now, what is that supposed to mean?" she asked herself.

For the next hour she tossed about, pondering that question, until at last she fell again into a dreamless sleep.

♦ ♦ ♦

That night he dreamt of Jan.

He dreamt of her vividly, tenderly. In this dream he could see her clearly and she was with him, loving him, and he loving her. It was not in any real sense an erotic dream, but it was a highly emotional one. The feelings that the dream aroused set the mood for him as the new day began. He awoke, acutely aware of the difference between her presence in the room during the dream and the empty place beside him now.

Again he felt the overwhelming pain of having lost her. If he had in fact become a non-person through some great cosmic accident, as seemed more and more probable, how could he expect she would or could be his wife? He had to face the possibility that she was married to someone else, had two, three, five children and was supremely happy in the life that had become hers without him.

Yesterday as he had driven down the highway through Fresno and toward Henley, he had planned to spend today here and perhaps tomorrow, and then drive to Lakeland, the church that he had served just out of seminary. Finally he had projected going from there to his student charge, the little crossroads of Arlando, where he had first begun to preach.

Now he was not so sure.

What could he possibly learn in the high resort country where he and Jan had spent those first years in full-time service? That the people there also did not recognize him and had neither record nor remembrance of his ever having been there? The only thing he had learned in Henley was that the pattern of change and differentiation was holding true. It would probably be wise to keep to the schedule and the plan that he had set for himself; but on this morning, with the feelings that his dream had aroused still strong within him, he could not argue himself into holding to his course. He wanted to go back home to San Diego, where both he and Jan had been born and had grown up, gone to school, met, loved, and married. Whatever awaited discovery at Lakeland would still be there when he got around to visiting later. But he had to have some answers about Jan and whether there could be any life with her.

What was God's will, he wondered. The thought called him to prayer and he centered down to praise readily, but try as he might, he felt no particular word forthcoming. If there was to be any direction this morning, he had to believe it had already come in the dream that so richly colored his outlook. Quickly he picked up the phone and called the Fresno Airport for reservations on the morning flight to San Diego. That done, he packed his bag and hurried to check out of the motel.

Breakfast came at the airport cafe while awaiting the plane that would take him back home, and by mid-morning he found himself high above the arid hinterlands of Southern California approaching Lindbergh Field, the municipal airport serving the teeming metropolis of San Diego.

By the time he had landed, deplaned, claimed his luggage and hired the new rental car to replace the one he had surrendered in Fresno, it was almost noon.

Nothing seemed to have changed here in the city of his birth, and yet he realized he would find again all remembrance of himself gone from the lives of people he might have counted on to welcome, recognize, and even to house him. He drove out to the main motel strip in Mission Valley north of the city and checked into a quiet but well appointed room.

Quickly he opened the telephone directory in the nightstand drawer underneath the telephone, and turned impatiently through the pages until he came to the name he sought: "McQueen..." There were several listings. There was no "Jan McQueen." His heart sank. But there was a "McQueen, J.E." Breathlessly, he punched in the numbers on the telephone keypad and waited. The telephone rang once, twice, three times. Would it be answered? Would it be Jan? Or would it be quite another McQueen? He could not believe that having married she would ever divorce and take back her maiden name. Seven, eight, nine. It was obvious now that the phone would not be answered. He let it ring several times more before he slowly slid the telephone back into its cradle.

What now? He glanced at his watch: 1:38 P.M. on Tuesday, the 17th of April. A sudden thought crossed his mind. Yesterday had been the last day to file an income tax return for last year. He had, as a matter of fact, done his own return on the last day of March and duly sent it in; but that was before the *Event* and doubtless he was as much an un-person to the Internal Revenue Service now as he was to everyone else. He had no doubt, in the eyes of the federal tax agents, he had never filed a tax return in his life and their computers had no record of him. But since he had no knowledge of any money he had in fact earned last year in the world as he now found it, he did not see how he could possibly file a return for last year, either now or a year from now. But this was no time to be sitting around considering such unimportant things. He needed some answers he could not get anywhere else. He slipped on his coat, straightened his tie, and left the motel unit, locking the door behind him. Starting his car, he turned it back toward downtown and the County Building where all the records were kept.

Twenty minutes later found him in the Recorder's Office for San Diego County, asking for certified copies of the records there. He put in his request for a copy of his own birth certificate, his parents' marriage license, or any records pertaining either to his father, Lewis

Allen Masters, or to his mother, Alice Lorraine Wexler, who had been married in this county on July 22, 1938. The clerk took the several official requests for information and retired to the computer room where the records were kept. After she had gone, John thought suddenly of seeking the birth records and other data on Jan Eileen McQueen, born in San Diego on September 14, 1948. Another clerk seemed willing to find such records for him, so he filled in the forms and leaned back to wait.

It seemed as if the wait would never end. The results came back, first of all on Jan. There was a certified record of her birth, as expected, but beyond the simple notations that previous copies of her birth certificate had been required on three distinct occasions, there was no record in the computer of any marriage license or other official notation on her (such as a certificate of death.) As far as this county knew, at any rate, she seemed to be alive and unmarried.

At length the primary courier returned; there was indeed a record of the birth of a John Lewis Masters on his remembered birth date. (Wes' connections had indeed done their job.) But there was no record or other mention of a Lewis Allen Masters, nor of a marriage involving any such person. With regard to Alice Lorraine Wexler, she was born on May 19, 1915 in Julian, California, and the records showed she had married Jacob R. Liebmann on June 12, 1945. A final entry showed a death certificate had been issued regarding her on June 13, 1949 as the result of a motorcycle accident. She seemed to have no children, having died "without issue."

It dawned on John that he was not, in fact, the un-person; rather he was the son of the un-person. It was his father who had disappeared from the place he ought to have occupied, and his own lack of place derived from being the son of a man who had never existed here.

Somehow the *Event* had cut short or turned aside the life of his father. Born in Ridgeham, New York some eighty-four years ago, he had grown up in the home of a volatile and sometimes brutal man, the oldest of two sons and a daughter. At the age of nineteen he had run away from home and enlisted in the Navy, where he had served for twelve years, rising to the rank of Chief Petty Officer. Many were the tales he had told in his son's hearing of life in the service in the years between the two World Wars. It was while he was stationed at the Naval Base at San Diego that he had met and fallen in love with Alice Wexler, the youngest daughter of a farming family in Julian, some sixty miles east of San Diego. She had come to the city seeking first, education, and then employment and had become a bookkeeper for a local contracting firm. Allen was thirty and Alice twenty-seven when they first met, and their courtship had its ups and downs; but love conquers all and they were married in a small Episcopal Church on the twenty-second of July, 1944.

John Lewis Masters, their only child, had been born into and grown up in a family that had little concern for Christ or the church. His parents had loved him and each other, but neither of them had ranked "religion" high on their list of priorities. The early habit the family had formed was to go each weekend to Julian to visit "the Ranch" where Alice's brother maintained the family orchards. When his uncle and aunt had sold the Ranch and moved to San Diego themselves, this way of life came to an end. That left the Masters family at home on Sunday at a time when John could become involved in Sunday School. At the invitation of a schoolmate he began attending a nearby Methodist church. At first he went only when the family had nothing better on its Sunday Morning agenda, but the longer he went the more interested John became. His parents acquiesced to this new involvement for their son and made room for it in family plans, so John became more and more regular and involved in church.

When John was fifteen his father had a stroke, and the shadow of early death loomed over him. John had to grow up quickly and assume more and more responsibility. He had worked hard to relieve the pressures on his parents, and after several months the elder Masters had returned to work.

John had just completed his second year at Hilltop Theological Seminary when his father suffered a heart attack and died within a few moments of being stricken. His mother was well-employed and he was himself married and serving the church in Arlando so the pattern and direction of his life was not greatly diverted, though he had felt deeply the loss of his father.

Alice Wexler Masters had continued to work until her retirement and had continued to live quietly in the family home until her death after a short illness just four years ago.

But the records now proved conclusively none of this had ever happened. Allen Masters had not married Alice. She had married someone else and had died without ever giving birth. He did not exist, nor was there any person analogous to himself in existence in the world as it now was.

So nothing pertaining to him or anything he had ever done or caused to happen remained. All of the things he could remember doing were left undone or had been accomplished in perhaps another time and way and place by someone else. He had, in fact, ceased to exist and it was as if he had never been; except that he was, and he did exist.

Whatever the *Event* might be that had caused this whole transformation, it had somehow left him in existence with his memories intact. Insofar as he could discover, this world was very close to that world where he had played his part, and he and his family were apparently the only variations from what had come to be. Were there others like him, as a consequence of the *Event* that he postulated must have taken place? He could imagine other lost souls wandering over the face of the landscape, looking for a past that had never been.

He had awakened two weeks ago this morning in Denver, clothed in the dress and aspect of a piece of human flotsam; a homeless indigent perhaps, unwashed and probably alcoholic, and lost. Had he died in that alleyway instead of waking up to self-discovery and renewed life, no one would have been surprised nor even noticed that he had, in fact, no past or known identity. Nor would anyone have mourned. Whatever had happened to remove his place in the world, he had been slipped back into a place that would cause no notice at all.

If there were others like him, would they also be found in downtown alleys, hunched against skid-row doorways? He knew himself blessed indeed to have found the kind of recognition and support that had happened for him. And this was only because he knew enough to talk to a pastor and be able to convince him that the particular piece of effluvia wandering into his church was, in fact, more than he appeared on the surface.

It was obvious that he had achieved no real answers yet to any question he was asking; rather, he had just come to know the dimension and the phrasing of the necessary question itself.

What had happened to sponge out the known life of Lewis Allen Masters and, by doing so, had almost destroyed the life of his son, yet had left that son here and remembering?

TWENTY-FIVE

♦

It was just five-thirty as John paused at the phone booth inside the entrance to the county building and again dialed the number for "McQueen, J.E." that he had called from his motel room earlier in the day. He let the signals in his ear indicate ten rings before he replaced the phone on its chrome holder and reclaimed the money. He walked briskly to his car and got in.

If that was Jan and she was at work, then in all probability she would just be getting off and leaving for home about now. If he drove to that address from here he might well get there at the same time or, more probably, shortly after her arrival. He made himself start the car and then, slowly, deliberately and carefully, backed out and headed toward the eastern and residential section of metropolitan San Diego.

On impulse, he found himself driving through the neighborhood where Jan had lived with her parents so long ago. As he came near the end of a particular block, he slowed and examined carefully the last building. In former days, it had been a combination Mom and Pop grocery and private residence, the place where Jan had grown up. It looked as he expected it to look. Both of her parents had died, and the building was now a fancier and newly remodeled home. Had he come back last year, it would not have appeared differently. He turned back toward his original destination.

For the next twenty minutes he drove with care and intentional restraint through the familiar streets. Many things he saw tested his memory, but he saw nothing he could be sure he would not have seen a month previously. Cities are alive and are constantly changing. Like the human body itself, old cells were being changed and sloughed off

106

and new cells were constantly being grown to take their places; so buildings were renewed, reoccupied, remodeled, redecorated, or torn down to be replaced by some new structure, idea, design, or function.

At length he turned into the quiet side street indicated by the address in the telephone directory and drove slowly the two short blocks to the garden apartments containing the number listed. He parked his car and walked slowly toward the designated door.

Was J. E. McQueen in fact his own Jan Eileen McQueen? He could hope so and tell himself it was likely, but he could not repress his doubts. He recalled the many times since their marriage when he had looked at his wife and tried to discover how he had had the good fortune to be married to such a beautiful person. Physical beauty was hers to a truly striking degree, but also a laughing simplicity and openness and trust that made her beautiful through and through. He really had never been able ever to understand how he had been the one she had loved and had chosen to marry when she could have had so many other husbands of greater appearance, prominence and promise.

But he did not exist. He had never existed. How could Jan not be married to someone after all this time? She would after all be forty-one this year and they would have been married for twenty-one years next December 28th. Now he had not married her in that ceremony with Christmas overtones in the sanctuary of the Adams Avenue Methodist Church all those years ago, and could it be even remotely thinkable she had not found someone else with whom to share her life and naturally affectionate nature? Probably this listing was just a cruel coincidence. The door would likely as not be opened by James Eugene McQueen, a crotchety bachelor angered at the disturbance of his routine preparations for his sparse evening meal.

With determination he pressed the doorbell button and held it. He could hear the chimes echo through the apartment. He listened for answering movement, but a passing car masked any possibility of being sure what he might have heard. The door remained closed. He rang again. No sound. No movement. No one yet at home. He looked at the door and its surroundings for some clue to the nature of its occupant. The worn typed label above the bell button read simply "J. E. McQueen" and the mailbox was a slot in the door, closed by a spring-loaded brass cover. No personalized welcome mat gave any clue. He turned and walked down the sidewalk, pausing after a few steps to look back through the window into the living room. The furniture was simple and nondescript, and did not tell him anything. Then, as he was about to turn back to the pathway to his car, his eye caught sight of a Vaseline-glass cruet standing on a shelf on the far side of the room. His heart leapt within him because he recognized this as having been a unique and prized possession of his late mother-in-law, and something that also meant a great deal to his wife. He suddenly felt confident this was, in fact, her apartment.

He got back into his car and sat thinking. He might sit here for hours before she came home. Indeed, she might not be in town at all; she could be away. His stomach was telling him he had eaten nothing since the jumbled excuse for a meal before the flight down. It made sense to go and eat somewhere nearby and then to return when she had had a chance to get home from wherever she was and whatever she had been doing. He started the engine and eased the car out and down the block. He drove to the main arterial and then along it until he found a popular restaurant. He parked and went inside. He could have had a place at once at the counter, but he made himself wait for a single table, and then ordered and ate in as slow and time-consuming fashion as he could. At length he emerged from this self-imposed exercise in patience and restraint, and drove back to the apartment.

Night had fallen and the other apartments in the building were lighted and busy, but the one belonging to Jan was still dark and quiet. On the off-chance she had returned and was in some room not visible from the front, he went up and rang the bell; but when this produced again no response he returned to his car to wait. He turned on the radio and sat back, trying to relax.

He had been fortunate enough once to have won her love. Even if she was single now, what made him think she would in fact choose him again? They had had a fine marriage, a happy companionship and joy in being together in all things (or almost all) but this had grown up in the two decades since that Sunday afternoon ceremony. At the beginning they had had their ups and downs, their doubts and disappointments. Living with another human being always took some getting used to, and life in the pressure-cooker of a church parsonage in a student charge did not make it any easier. In fact, if they had not been committed as Christians to making the best of their marriage no matter what, with no possibility open to either of them to do anything else, it might not have held together at all. John knew his wife had felt most deeply the lack of children, and this had been a source of unrest in their relationship for some time. He knew he had made things worse by being the self-satisfied husband, who thought in those early days that the marriage had taken place to care for him and to meet his needs and satisfy his desires. It had taken him many years to discover the real secret of marriage. But their relationship had grown and blossomed and become that one-ness of which The Creator spoke and The Apostle preached. They had indeed become "one nephesh," one united being together.

He could recall that night just a few years ago when he had looked across the room at Jan as she sat reading quietly beside the fire in their Lakeland Parsonage and had realized, with a start, this was not the woman he had married. The Jan he had married with such delight and confidence turned out to be a stranger, with unsuspected values and expectations and sometimes unpredictable behavior. But that troublesome wife had, in turn, all but vanished. In her place was one who was so much a part of himself that in order for him to be whole and integrated and fully alive she had to be present and sharing in every situation with him.

Now the work of those years, the joy of that love they had permitted God to fashion in them, was gone, wiped out by the *Event*. Could he indeed hope it might somehow be recovered after so many years of differing experience and starting from such an unpromising place? He put his head back and closed his eyes and prayed.

Cars came and went, some stopping here and there on the block, their lights always bringing his attention back to the possibility that this might be the time when he would see her again. Each time he was disappointed.

The car radio turned from music to what was called "classic radio," specifically an old "Dragnet" adventure. John made himself listen and became vicariously involved in the problems facing Joe Friday. The only real mystery was how they managed to get so many commercials crammed into what had once been a largely uninterrupted story.

The felon detected, arrested and convicted, the radio returned by way of five minutes of late news to music once more. Activity had diminished on the street now. The cars were noticeably fewer and some lights were going out in surrounding residences. John looked at his watch. It was ten o'clock. A car turned onto the street two blocks down and drove slowly toward him. Just beyond his own car it slowed down, and swerved to the curb. A lithe figure emerged from the passenger side and, after some words through the open door with the driver, closed it and walked quickly up the walk, reaching into a purse to retrieve a key. The figure paused at the door, the door opened, and light streamed through the opening as the person disappeared into the room before the door closed.

She had come home. Jan was now just a few steps away from where he sat. He pictured in his mind what would happen now: He would go up and ring the bell. She would come to the door and carefully look outside to see who it was at this late hour. She would, of course, not recognize him. How could he explain to her who he was? He thought about the pain of that flat unresponsive stare he had experienced so often lately from those whom he knew and loved and had treasured. This would be the worst of all. Already he felt the pain of her unknowing and tried to picture how she would react. Suspicion, fear, anger at being disturbed by a stranger at this time of night? All of these possibilities stabbed at him with pain he could not endure.

Abruptly he decided not to risk it. Having found her, he would go and find out more about her situation. Then he would become acquainted in a less painful and "more natural" way and see what might develop. He wished he might have seen for certain who it was that had brought her home.

He started the engine, then turned it off again.

No.

He could not live with himself if he drove away from here now like a coward. He laid his head on the steering wheel and prayed, giving to God his love and Jan and all things, for the doing of His will. Thus strengthened and steeled, he got out and walked up the sidewalk to the doorway.

Yet again he rang the bell.

This time there was movement. Footsteps coming to the other side of the door. The porch light came on and he could hear the safety chain being inserted in the door. Then the door opened to the limit of the chain and her voice said, "Yes?"

He couldn't think of what to say. How could he explain his presence here and who he was? He had to say something.

So he did.

He simply spoke her name: "Jan..."

She looked at him through the opening beside the door. He could see her beautiful face sandwiched between door and jamb. Her eyes flicked over his face and into his eyes. They got very large and then closed, as soundlessly she lost consciousness and sank to the floor in a dead faint.

TWENTY-SIX

♦

The next few seconds were violent and confused. John placed his shoulder against the door and thrust with his whole strength. The screws holding the chain were torn out and the door swung back explosively to admit him. He scooped up the unconscious woman and carried her to the couch, carefully putting her down and beginning to rub her hands and gently pat her cheeks.

In a few moments she began to stir and opened her eyes.

"Jan, I'm sorry. Believe me; I didn't think it would be like this."

She still seemed dazed.

"Who are you? Where have you been? Who are you? Where have you been?" Jan repeated over and over.

John put his arm around her and helped her to sit up. She did not shrink from his touch, indeed she seemed to welcome and even expect it.

"Who am I? Where have I been? I am not sure I should try to answer either of your questions right now. Until about two weeks ago I thought I was a United Connectional minister and the husband of the finest wife a man ever had, the former Jan McQueen. Then, suddenly, my whole life seemed to explode like an overage bubble, and I find myself in a world where no one has ever heard of me or seen me before."

He watched her eyes for the dawning of disbelief, but saw none. Quickly he began to tell her of his latest memories and of the things that had begun to happen after his awakening in Denver.

From time to time in his narrative she nodded. Her eyes seemed to rest as hungrily on him as his did upon her. He talked of his feelings at being unrecognized by those to whom he had ministered and with

112

whom he had once shared; and he spoke of the fears he had felt in approaching her. He steeled himself for the question he had to ask.

"Jan, do you recognize me? Have you ever seen me before?"

Her whole expression radiated joy as she answered. "Oh yes. Again and again. Night after night, when I was younger. Over and over again I dreamed of you. Vividly. Warmly. You were always so tender, so thoughtful. I guess I had the first dream when I was about twelve. Not always the same. Sometimes doing the crazy things together you do only in dreams. Sometimes quite ordinary dreams of doing ordinary things. Once or twice my dream was pretty exciting sexually, as I dreamt you were making love to me. Nothing ever felt guilty or wrong. Mostly the dream was a time for feeling great love and peace and contentment. I don't think a week has gone by when I haven't dreamt of you, and those were always the best nights of my life. In high school it happened every night, and the guys I met at school were nothing when compared to the love I shared with you in my dreams. And it was you. I always could see you so clearly, so vividly; and you always looked just as I saw you a few minutes ago on the porch. My parents thought I was crazy and tried to get me interested in some flesh-and-blood possibilities, but I could never make myself become really interested. Oh, I went out. But always after a date I would come home and dream of you, and the contrast was too great for the relationship to survive. I have really waited for you all my life."

She threw back her head and laughed. "And here you are. You are real." She was blinking back tears.

Tenderly he took her hands in his own. "Jan, in my life as it was I have been married to you for more than twenty years, and I love you so I cannot bear trying to live without you. But my life is in ruins. The only thing I want to do, the one thing I know how to do, is ministry. But I don't see how a man without background, respectable past, degree, or ordination is going to get back to caring for the souls of people. I don't have anything to offer you but faith in God and the trust of a few friends who have come to believe in me in spite of all appearances. That is all I have in the world. But I can't think of you as anything but my wife, and I have to ask you to marry me—and to do so right away."

Jan laughed. "What else can I do? I obviously cannot marry anyone else. You have seen to that by haunting my dreams and driving off all the competition. My answer is 'yes', sealed with a kiss."

John kissed Jan for the first time in this new world as his intended bride.

All thought of weariness or sleep had fled from them both. They sat and talked as if they had known each other forever. Jan wanted to hear all John had to say of his memories of their marriage and what they had done together. He hungered for all the facets of the life that she had lived while waiting to discover the one of whom she had so constantly dreamed.

So they talked and laughed and kissed until they became aware the night had passed and dawn had come. Dancing in joy about the kitchen, Jan fixed a first breakfast for her love and they ate lightly of what John felt to be the finest meal that ever was. At nine o'clock Jan called in to her job at the library as "sick," and they discussed what they might do with the day.

"What kind of wedding do you want?" John asked his irrepressible fiancée.

She laughed. "A quick one. A Christian one. No frills. No one else. Just us."

"Are you willing to tarnish your reputation enough to be married right away, today—this morning?" John was smiling yet serious.

"What do you mean?"

"Well, a regular marriage license takes several days, mostly for the taking and evaluation of the blood test. If you are willing to confess we have already been acting like old married people and have in fact so represented ourselves, we can, by the laws of California, be married with a 'confidential license' that requires no blood test and can take place as soon as we can find a minister. All we need is one who will be willing to take the time necessary to 'set matters right' for us, so we can be husband and wife."

Jan grinned at him. "Why not? My reputation is shot anyway. After all, a man stayed over with me alone in my apartment last night. And besides, the things that you have sometimes done with me in my dreams justify my demanding to be made an honest woman several times over."

So eleven o'clock found them, freshened and dressed in their best, standing before the once familiar altar of the Adams Avenue United Connectional Church while Jan's bewildered pastor read the marriage service to a perfect stranger and a fine unmarried woman in his congregation whom he had always thought to be the very pillar of chastity and virtue. They had presented the special and confidential marriage license and, by doing so, had confessed love and intimacy and *de facto* marriage, so he could do nothing else but perform the ceremony they requested. He would then complete the form and mail it in for "recording under seal." It was strange. Never had he been so dismayed at performing a service for a parishioner, and yet never had he felt so much joy in the room and felt so right in what he was doing.

For John's part, he could not help remembering standing with this same Jan before the same altar, hearing those same words. But then there had been a whole congregation, including both his parents and hers. How he wished that might have been the case, but he would settle for what he now had.

Finally the stranger kissed his beautiful bride and they embraced the startled pastor, gave him a generous honorarium, left an offering for the church and departed.

The pastor went back to his study and mulled over the event. It had always been a mystery why such a beautiful woman had remained unmarried. When he had called on her, there had been no hint of anything amiss. Now she confessed, with no apparent shame at all, she had been sharing her life with this man—a man who seemed to know more about the proper routine of such a marriage than he did himself. Well, it was none of his business now and he was happy he could help make things right and give them so much obvious joy.

Back at her apartment, John carried his wife over the threshold. Jan put her feet down, got her balance and drew John close to her.

"This whirlwind courtship is beginning to take its toll. I think we ought to get some rest."

John kissed her in agreement.

Jan drew him by the hand into the bedroom. She began to unbutton her dress. "We have no children, you said. Do you think it is too late for us to try again?"

John showed he did not think so.

And for the second time in his life he found her to be a virgin.

TWENTY-SEVEN

◆

The week that followed was a busy one.

Jan gave up her job at the library on the shortest of notices and found this was not resented because Mrs. Winthrop, the branch Librarian, had been wrestling with the urgent necessity of reducing costs by letting one employee go. She was relieved someone had voluntarily stepped out, though she was dismayed that it was the pleasant efficiency she knew as Jan.

But when John had gone out to feed the parking meter, Grace appeared and drew Jan into a corner. "Jan, you have been holding out on me. Here I was trying to help you and making a fool of myself by urging Jerry upon you—and you had John hidden somewhere all the time. I really think you should have been straight with me."

Jan smiled and took her hand. "Grace, I am really sorry, but there was nothing else I could do." She thought for a moment about how she might say something to ease the other woman's visible disappointment, without telling an untruth.

"You see, I really never expected to have John ever come back into my life. I didn't think he would possibly reappear; but I have always loved him. And when he came for me after all, and there he was—what else could I do? He loves me as much as I love him."

Grace withdrew her hand. "Just as long as you are happy, Jan. That is what counts," she said stiffly, turning away. She walked over behind the desk and busied herself with the computer there.

Jan gathered her few belongings, said goodbye to them once more, and went out to where John waited in the car.

With the distractions of her job out of the way, she entered into the full-time task of becoming wife and companion to her marvelously affectionate husband. It was like those dreams from which she had awakened so many times before; and she had to keep testing and reassuring herself that this was, in fact, real. She had really found and married the one whom she had always been seeking. It was a time of joy and adventure.

Jan had always thought, when she permitted herself to think about it, that if she did marry after all these years the adjustment would be difficult and even doubtful of success. She had been prepared to encounter demands and attitudes that she would not easily be willing to accept. What she had found instead were tenderness, understanding, and unanticipated sensitivity on the part of her husband. She found that this generated in her an overflowing determination to give love even more abundantly than she was receiving it. And so, day by day, the joy and contentment mounted; and she was happier than she had ever thought possible.

They did everything together. She went with John to the Naval District Headquarters while he made application for information on the enlistment of Lewis Allen Masters. John told the truth, if not the whole truth (for who could begin to believe his story?). He represented himself as an orphan whose father was said to have been in the Navy from 1935 to 1945, having enlisted in New York State, and about whom his lost son was seeking whatever information he might glean. The officer took the information without making any promises and told him to come back in perhaps a week to find out what Washington had dredged from its archives.

A telephone call summoned them back after only four days. No record had been unearthed at the Pentagon—either in those records that had been entrusted to the computer or in the still-existing accumulation of old files of alphabetized yellowing paper—of any Allen Lewis Masters. There seemed no possibility for error: no man of that name had ever served for any period in the United States Navy. The officer seemed genuinely distressed to be casting aspersions upon the truthfulness of his assumed father, and John found himself reassuring the man of his own acceptance and continuing confidence that some suitable explanation would be found. He could not tell him that he, himself, was similarly displaced from a fair assemblage of computer tapes, disks, and drives, and from a scattered acre of filing cabinets. He

117

thanked the Navy vicariously for its united effort and departed.

That had happened on Monday morning. It was a fitting anticlimax to the preceding day, the first Sunday John and Jan had spent together in their new married life.

They had returned for the eleven o'clock service to the Adams Avenue Church, to the initial discomfiture of its pastor. He was obviously quite surprised to see them approaching the front door as he stood there on the steps, welcoming the earlier arrivals of his flock before the prelude called him to make last-minute preparation for his responsibilities in leading worship. Having greeted the newlyweds with an enthusiasm he did not quite feel (because of his continuing questions about their moral conduct before last Wednesday's ceremony) his eyes grew wide with surprise to hear Jan introduce her new husband to a longtime Sunday school classmate standing nearby as "the Reverend John Masters." This was the first definite word he had heard that this man was a clerical colleague (though as he looked back on it there had been hints aplenty) and he tried to accommodate this new intelligence with the premarital conduct implied by the license by which they had been united. Well, whatever the precise truth might be, there could be no question they were in fact duly and properly married now, and he could clearly see Jan was even more beautiful in her radiant happiness than she had been before. He thought to himself he would inquire into the church and denomination of this "brother pastor" when the opportunity presented itself.

Meanwhile Jan was enjoying the reactions of her various church friends and acquaintances to her newly married state and husband. Over and over again she had to apologize gently to this one and that for not inviting them to attend the ceremony, explaining they had decided on marriage so abruptly there was no time for invitations and guests or any of the usual public display such occasions were thought to require. Several times that morning before church the question (variously phrased) was asked, "how long have you known each other?" and Jan's answer "I've known and loved him all my life, since I was twelve years old" surprised those who up until last week would have thought they were close enough to the mysteriously unmarried Jan McQueen to know whether she had any serious men-friends at all.

With the first notes of the prelude, the newlyweds made their way to a pew halfway down on the pulpit side and, sitting close beside each other, began to prepare themselves to worship God as husband and wife. Both had a lifetime of worship experience and had no trouble centering on the awareness of God's Presence in this place, and both found they had much to express in terms of praise and thanksgiving to God for His goodness and for the great blessings they had received this week. Indeed, the flood of joyful prayer had not begun to abate when it was stemmed by the beginning of the worship service planned for the congregation and led by the pastor.

It was a rich service for John. Having conducted worship for so long, it was still a rare experience for him to have the luxury of sitting quietly in a pew and focusing his whole attention on God and on the Word being proclaimed. The contrast between this morning and that painful and confusion-racked experience just a week ago in Centerville was so great he found it difficult to keep his joy from spilling out into audible praise.

This was now the fourth Sunday since *the Event* had thrust him into bewildering exile from the world that made some provision for him, and at last he had a place once again. Whatever else might happen, he now belonged where he was—sitting beside his wife. She had been his greatest loss, but now bleakest tragedy had been averted and that loss restored. He found he could entirely trust God in both intellect and feelings with all that yet needed to happen, because of His manifest providence in restoring Jan to him.

Never had John been so acutely aware of the Presence and Love of God. Never had he attended any service when the Holy Spirit was more forcefully present. The prayers, the hymns, the scripture lessons, and the sermon were filled with words, phrases, and invitations to insight that filled his being with the belief that his life, no matter how uprooted he felt, was clearly in the hands of His Creator and all would be restored and made even better than the life that he had lost. All that was required was he should trust and be open to God's guidance and grace on a moment-by-moment basis and obedient to all God would make known to him of The Divine Will for the united life that he and Jan now shared once again.

It is doubtful if anyone else in that church service came away so convinced of its inspiration and power as did John Masters and his wife. If they had been less caught up in the true worship and praise of God, they might have found the liturgy quite usual and the sermon routine and minimally inspiring and inspired. It is true in worship particularly, as it is in faith generally, that you receive what you are expecting; and this couple were so blessed in each other and in what the past few days had brought that they mounted from strength to strength and heard not what a man had assembled, but what the Spirit of God could say through the most ordinary words. John had often publicly stated that the words he spoke in preaching were of minimal importance because the Holy Spirit gave them personal meaning and content for each listener, according to his or her needs. So, far from everyone hearing the same sermon, there were as many sermons preached on Sunday in a given church as there were persons gathered and spiritually ready to hear. Never had this been more true than it was for them this day.

The service ended. As the organ postlude wound to its unheeded conclusion, a cluster of Jan's friends who had arrived for church after the prelude had started and had not heard the good news of her marriage or seen the newly installed husband, descended upon them and gathered for introduction and to tender congratulations. It was therefore some minutes after silence had come to the sanctuary that John and Jan were free to start walking out.

Look.

John turned his head. Three pews back, next to the window, a woman was still seated, bowed forward in an attitude of continuing prayer. Jan's eyes went to her husband's face and then to the figure he was looking at. Jan saw the slight trembling of the shoulders and whispered, "She's crying."

John nodded. Without a word they made their way across the now empty pews just ahead of the distressed figure and stopped in front of her. Jan laid her hand gently on the sobbing shoulder.

"Mabel, what is it? What's wrong? Can we help?"

The tear-streaked face looked up. "It's Jim, my son. He's—Oh God, he's into drugs. Friday night I found them in his room. I wasn't really looking, you understand. I just took some shirts in and while putting them away I found it. I was so hurt and so angry—and so afraid. When I confronted him he blew up and threw some things together and left. He's gone, left home—and I'm so frightened. Why did this have to happen? Where did I fail? Oh God—" and she wept once more.

Jan felt completely at a loss in the situation. What could they say? What was there to do? She looked at John, expecting to see him share her own feelings and expression of helplessness. But he was looking intently at the woman. Even as Jan watched his mouth began to form words, at first so faint as to be inaudible, but then quickly louder and louder.

"Thus says the Lord: I have heard your prayer and know your grief, and your son is under My Hand. I have set about him a hedge of thorns to separate him from those who would lead him from My path. Be at peace. Your son will be restored to you this very day. Only love and trust. Trust him and trust Me. Your soul shall be delighted in the goodness of love and the rightful pride of a mother in her son." The last sentences were vibrant in sound and in promise.

The woman was quiet now, smiling through the wetness of her grief. It was clear she had heard and understood and was accepting the words spoken to her as true and promising. "Thank you," she whispered, and wiping her eyes quickly with her hands, got up and hurried away.

Jan turned to her husband. "Why did you say those things? What will happen if they don't work out?" She was clearly upset.

John looked back at his troubled bride, wanting to smile and yet realizing this would seem to treat her sincere concern with less seriousness than it deserved.

"Jan, I said those things to her because God was saying them to me. Believe me, I did not want to say anything to her when we came over, but the Holy Spirit had a word for her and I was the one He chose to speak it."

"And you are sure it will come true for her? She won't be disappointed?"

"I am sure it was truly God's word for her at this moment, and I was commanded to speak just what I spoke. We have been obedient and God will honor His word; we can leave that to Him."

Thoughtfully Jan took his hand, and they made their way back to the center and walked toward the front door. The pastor was occupied with some urgent parishioners and nodded to them across his involvement as they passed and went down the front steps and out of the building. For some moments they walked in the warm sunshine without speaking. Finally Jan broke the silence.

"I have never seen anything like that before in my life. I have never actually seen someone speak under the power of God. It may take some getting used to."

John turned and flashed his familiar grin. "Believe me, dearest, you never get used to it—at least I have not. But you come at least to accept it and rejoice when you are part of its happening.

TWENTY-EIGHT

◆

Jan and John spent that Sunday afternoon exploring the places in San Diego associated with his memories of the life that was. They drove to his old neighborhood and parked near the house from which he was born and where he could remember growing up. They strolled about the neighborhood while he recalled stories of people he had known and events that had taken place in this house or on that lot. They climbed a small hill and came to the school John remembered attending. He told her about his memories of going to school for the first time and his mother's practice of bringing to school a packed lunch when it was raining and he could not be expected to walk the three blocks home for his noon meal. They laughed together about those tuna salad sandwiches made with hamburger buns and braced with strong, sweet hot chocolate. He told of his tenth birthday, when his father met him after school at the entrance to the school grounds with a new bicycle that he had then learned to ride with his dad's help that very afternoon. He told her about his best friends in school and what he could recall had happened to them.

As they walked they fell into a deep discussion about John's friends and how much might in fact have changed in their lives from what he remembered because he had not participated in them—could not have done so in the world as it now was. Were there some of his friends who had been injured or perhaps crippled or even killed because of his not being there to do something that he had done in his own experienced childhood? He remembered George Drake, in Centerville and told Jan of seeing alive again a man he could remember burying. She was curious about the linkage through which he showed how this could

123

be possible, and then was both intrigued and dismayed to find it had been her own activities in that other life which had caused the chain of events leading to what must now be judged George's premature death.

So it might well be that some of those with whom he could remember going to school would have had their lives changed for the better by his absence, while others would have suffered from the void he might have filled. Had he come back to San Diego six months ago he would not have known how to get in touch with any of his classmates from that old elementary school. Of course, now the problem was compounded by the questions his inquiring as a stranger would raise. Besides, it would just add to the already abundant body of proof that no one had any knowledge or record of his existence.

They stopped on the sidewalk in front of his former home once more. John stood and looked at it, recalling all of the memories that had now apparently never taken place at all in that old structure. Here his father had died, suddenly and quietly. His mother had lived here until a few days before her death, when she had to be hospitalized. After the funeral he had sorrowfully cleared out the house and quickly sold it. Now it was, in fact, someone else's home without ever having been his at all. As he continued to gaze, the front door opened and a woman of about his age came down the walk.

"Is there something I can help you with?" she said.

"Why no, I don't believe so," John replied.

"I have been watching you staring at our home, and I did wonder if there was anything about it or about us that concerned you."

John smiled gently. "Let's just say I find this house very interesting, and it reminds me of a house I once knew very well."

"Oh, I see. Did you grow up nearby?"

"I think I grew up very far away. Thank you for your trouble anyway."

The woman turned to go and had taken several steps back toward her open door when John called out gently to her, "By the way, did you ever manage to deal with the settling problem and what it did to the doorway into the front bedroom from the living room?"

He turned and began to walk his wife back down the block to where their car was parked. Behind them the woman had turned, mouth opened wide in amazement. John glanced back at her, smiled, and then laughed softly to Jan. "She'll think about that for a while."

"But how could you be sure they would have had the same trouble with the house you did?"

"The difference, Jan, is in that thing I call 'The Event'—something that affected my father and perhaps some others, although I have no evidence about that. But as far as I have been able to tell, it did not have any general impact upon nature. So I assumed the same succession of dry seasons caused the same subsidence under the piling that supports that part of the house. They may have been no more noticing than we were until suddenly the door no longer fitted the doorway. I had to take steps to trim and rehang the door; either that or get in and somehow lift and support the house, far too much for me to attempt."

He opened the car door for his wife, saw her safely in, and then hurried around to climb in the driver's side. The engine roared to life and he eased out into traffic to make his way across town to San Diego State University, the place where John had first met and courted Jan in that life that they no longer shared. The campus was now a sprawling mixture of original buildings from his student days and the multitude of larger and more complex structures now struggling to accommodate the tens of thousands of students currently in regular attendance. They parked in a convenient corner of a gigantic empty parking lot and set out again on foot.

If Jan had any doubts about the accuracy of John's memories, those doubts were stilled by their hour of walking about the buildings that remained from their college experience. John's knowledge of the topography and existing buildings, of the make-up and foibles of the faculty, and of her own habits as an entering freshman convinced her that he had very special knowledge indeed.

At length they came to a flowery corner of a quadrangle in the older section of the college. John turned and took Jan in his arms.

"This was the place where I first told you I loved you."

"John, how I wish you had."

"Believe me, dearest, I did. I really did."

Jan looked down. "Oh John, I don't doubt it. But I was never there except perhaps in my dreams; and I wish I had been. I feel we have lost so much time. So much of our life together has been wasted by this— this thing you know to have happened and I just have to take on faith."

John was touched and serious. "There is one thing I have come to believe over the years I have served as a pastor and it stands me in good stead right now because I have to trust it is even more true than I thought. 'All things work together for good, to those who love God, who are called according to His purposes.' So what looks wasted right now must have some values that we will discover. Only, I guess I will be the only one to discover them because you will not have any way of knowing whether or not what is happening now is any different than what would have been happening. But the most important thing in the world to me right now is that I can stand right here and tell my wife I do love her."

Jan answered with a kiss.

It was now four weeks and four hours since his old life had ended and confusion had begun.

TWENTY-NINE

◆

They had dinner on Sunday evening in a fine and popular seafood restaurant overlooking the harbor for which San Diego is famous. It was necessarily a leisurely process because the place was so crowded, but John and Jan had nothing better to do than to be with each other. The time of waiting for a table and then being served when a large establishment was coping with its maximum business was unimportant and well spent as they talked and shared and laughed together. Now with the ample meal eaten and the coffee that would replace dessert about to be served, the press of arriving customers had abated and here and there tables sat empty for lack of those waiting to fill them. So they felt no pressure to finish quickly, and when the coffee came—rich, black, and hot—they drank it slowly and talked much.

It was Jan who brought the conversation back once again to the situation where they found themselves. "John, you said this afternoon there would be some good things that would come out of what has happened to you—or, I guess if you are right, to us. This is all so new to me, and I have no way of knowing what might be different or how it is different. Do you have any reason for knowing there are going to be real compensations, and if so, what do you think they may be?"

John reached under the table, sought her hand and held it. "I know how it must be, dearest. On Tuesday evening a complete stranger to your waking hours turns up on your doorstep and you admit him to your home and to your life. You do this only because he has been the star attraction of the most vivid dream—life anyone has ever heard of. Then this fellow tells you he has recently come from living with you for twenty-one years after a courtship and wedding that he remembers

127

and can describe in detail. As far as you know, it never really happened. You marry him and get swept up into his desperate efforts to make sense out of the sudden dislocation that he has suffered. So, as hard as you try to accept his word about the reality he has known and to think it is somehow true, you cannot honestly feel it is made of any other stuff than that of which your dreams were fashioned. Because, you know every day you have lived and can, if pressed, account for every hour. And none of the things he talks about ever really happened to you. You want to believe I am telling something that is somehow true, but your entire acceptance comes out of your desire to please and love the stranger you have married and find yourself loving."

Jan nodded.

John continued. "I told you earlier I am convinced there are going to be some advantages that will come out of this situation, out of *the Event* and its effects upon our lives. 'All things work together for good' we are promised, and I believe it. Not that all things are good. I don't find it good that my father has disappeared from the life that I knew him to have led, that my mother was in fact not my mother and instead of living to the rich old age that I remember, she died at thirty-four in an accident without ever having a child at all. It is not good that I find myself without any of the records required for employment in the profession to which I was and still am called. As a pastor, I am unemployable because I have not even officially graduated from high school, much less college or seminary. And it is not at all good that in your experience we were separated for the past two decades and you lived those years alone."

"The life that we had was not always blissful and it certainly was not without its moments of friction and distress for you, but on the whole I am sure you enjoyed the living of it. However, there may now be some advantage for you in coming into marriage with a man previously trained in the skills of being a husband by his former wife, who happens to have been yourself. You'll have to take my word for it that the young Jan McQueen did not find her husband to be as sensitive or as caring as you find yours to be, and it is she who paid the price of his apprenticeship in tears and argument and anger. A man can learn a lot in twenty years, and the thing that I learned most of all was how very much I loved my wife. When I lost her in the process of losing everything else, that was the greatest tragedy. You don't know, you cannot imagine how sure I was that you would naturally have found someone else to love and to marry; but how futile it seemed to want to do anything without you."

"Your dreams kept you for me. Whenever someone came near and began to open a pathway for love, that very vivid dream would recur and blight the waking feelings with emotions far deeper that hung on and colored the day even after you awakened. Isn't that so?"

"Yes, that was exactly the way it always happened. Somehow I could never be interested in him because he seemed so, well, so pale and lifeless when compared with the one in my dreams whom I knew I loved. It was really very strange and everyone was so upset and out of patience with me. I believed they were right but there was nothing I could do. However much I might think this new man was really a fine person and had all the necessary qualities for a serious relationship that would finally lead to marriage, I would have another dream and then I would hardly be able to be polite to him, he suffered so by comparison. Nobody understood and neither did I."

"But don't you see, Jan? This was not something you did, either consciously or subconsciously. You could not know that one day I would stand on your doorstep late at night, ringing your doorbell with the good news that I had in fact married you two decades before. And my wife of two months ago never said a word to anyone about ever having any special dreams after she was twelve years old. We had a true marriage, we had entered into that unique spiritual relationship, a oneness that is far deeper and more permanent than just some kind of contractual association and convenient agreement to live and work and share and sleep together. The Bible says when two people let God fulfill the reality of marriage in their lives they become one 'nephesh.' That is a Hebrew word that means 'living being' or perhaps 'personality' or 'soul.' Marriage is truly a God-given mystery, and since we had that then it was divinely preserved. Those dreams were sent by God Himself."

Jan withdrew her hand from his long enough to take a sip of coffee, then sought his hand once again. "But why didn't God do something to prevent whatever you are calling 'the Event?' Why couldn't we have been left to live that life? If God cared so much for our marriage, why did He let anything happen to it?"

"Don't you know this is the question I have asked over and over again? It is the human thing to ask. If God is good and loving and aware, then why does He ever permit suffering and accident and tragedy? We struggle with this question all our lives, and the lives of the saints are filled with the same consideration right back to the Bible itself. This is the question dealt with in the 73rd Psalm, in the Book of Job, and supremely in the Cross of Christ. And the answer that we come up with is that God is not in the protection business, but rather is in the business of nurturing and raising up strong children of character who have learned to rely upon Him in all things and who have grown in power and purpose and understanding as a result of being sustained in trouble, rather than being protected from it. 'All things work together for good.' I rather picture God as a composer-conductor presiding over a symphony of lives, causing them to interact both in space and time to produce His masterpiece; that we of course from our place in the ensemble cannot understand or appreciate."

"But John, how can it possibly be that things are changed in time? What has happened has happened, and it cannot un-happen. The one thing we know is the past cannot be changed. Yet this 'Event' has uprooted your, our, past completely."

"I don't know. We are familiar with the things Einstein said about time, relating it to the spatial dimensions and in effect making time a function of space and material dimensions itself. We know time is thus part of this creation that God has wrought, and God Himself is outside of time as He is outside of space. We live in the midst of a theater of reality that was created to be our nurturing place; to our eyes it is unthinkably immense and complicated. We live on a small planet in a system around a moderately small sun as part of a swarm of stars swirling in a cloud called by us 'The Milky Way Galaxy.' We know this galaxy of which we are a part is only one of billions of such galaxies, little dancing puddles of stars separated from each other by an unthinkable gulf of virtual nothingness, with all moving away from a common point at which it is assumed they were all called into being some number of billions of years ago. The whole of reality is almost too great for our minds to grasp. And yet, this does not contain God but is rather an object of His fashioning, held in His hand if we are to think in a human way about the incomprehensible. This whole cosmic reality is no more to the God Who created it than is a ball of modeling clay to a child who is playing with it."

"So, as God stands outside of space He also stands outside of time. To God all time is *now* just as all space is *here*. For Him there is no past and no future; only a great mosaic of successive and related presents. So God began to send the dreams to your life well before you would ever have met me in the life we lived before *the Event*. From the beginning of the world God foresaw *the Event* and permitted it, seeing also that it would be turned to good effect in our lives, or would have that possibility, and it was somehow a natural part of the world fallen away from His perfection His children must be permitted to endure."

Jan sat staring across the shimmering bay. "How will our lives be in any way better than they would have been or, I guess, than they were?"

"That I don't really know yet; and if and when I do know, I will tell you. I do seem to be more aware of the leading of God and more open to His Spirit than I was before. My spiritual gift when I ministered before *the Event* was that of being a pastor-teacher. But in the past four weeks I have been involved in healing and prophecy in ways that were not part of my usual expectations before. They say 'God never closes a door but He opens another,' and I believe this will prove to be true, even if I cannot quite see more than a direction where to start groping for a doorknob.... ."

John had stopped in mid-sentence with his eyes riveted on a woman of his own age who was walking toward their table enroute to the exit. He muttered a confused, "Please excuse me" to his wife and arose to stand in the passageway blocking the progress of the woman and her escort.

"Pardon me, but don't I know you? Aren't you, weren't you, Elizabeth Warren?"

She stopped. "Why yes, I am. Do I know you?"

"I... I doubt it. No, you wouldn't have known me. I am just glad to see you looking so well."

"Well thank you, but there's no reason for me to be anything else. Now if you will excuse me."

John moved out of their way and they passed on, hardly delayed by the puzzling encounter.

Jan looked intently at her husband. "What was that all about?"

It was obvious John was puzzled and troubled. "She was a girl who lived down the block from me. One morning when we were both seventeen and juniors at San Diego High, she committed suicide. Killed herself with her father's pistol. And I cannot imagine how I fit in or why, after the Event, she is alive."

THIRTY

♦

They were in the car and driving out of the parking lot before the conversation resumed.

"She was a very pretty girl," John said, "and popular with the smooth guys and the athletes. She was not my type because I was quite sure she would find me boring and not worth cultivating. She was always working around or sunbathing outside in sun suits or bathing suits that kept my adolescent eyes busy looking. For a couple of years she was maybe the greatest problem I had in my Christian life, just because she was such an exciting neighbor. Then one morning there were police cars everywhere. It was drizzling and foggy and the red lights lit up the dreariness in a strange way we all noticed. I was getting ready for school, so mother went down the block and across the street to find out what was up. She came back with the news Elizabeth had not come home the night before, and after seeking her everywhere else they had found her out in a little tool shed behind the garage. The police said she had killed herself with a shot through the mouth into the brain sometime early the night before. I remember wondering why a pretty girl who was so popular and could have any guy she wanted would do something like that."

"And there has to be a connection with you?"

"In order for her to be alive now, I think there must be. It's hard to see any other explanation. But, for the life of me, I don't see what it could be."

"Was she pregnant?"

"What?"

Jan repeated. "Was she pregnant? Was she carrying a baby when she died?"

"Oh. I don't know. Yes, there were some whispers she might have been expecting. But you don't think..."

Jan laughed. "Not by just looking, no. I don't think you were the one responsible directly. But you must have been the one who somehow caused it, however indirectly."

"Yes, but how? She just barely knew I was alive. We would never even walk together when we came home on the same bus, and that didn't happen often. She would walk on ahead and I would follow."

"And look?"

"Knowing what I know now, I'd never give her a second glance."

Jan laughed, but continued, "And you never introduced anyone to her, suggested anyone take her out? No one came to visit you and discovered her and later on began to take her out?"

"So far as I know, none of those things happened. I cannot think of any direct link at all."

They drove together in silence.

"I think I have an idea that may help," Jan finally broke in. "Tomorrow, let's see if we can get your senior yearbook for San Diego High and go through to see if you can find anyone who should be there that is not."

"That's not the easiest thing in the world to do. My memory is far from perfect."

"Of course, but there is just a chance. I am guessing sometime earlier in your life your presence somehow kept someone in the picture with this girl that ultimately led to her downfall and despair and death. Without you, that person didn't continue in any relationship that could have permitted him to meet and finally mistreat her."

"You mean he might have died earlier if it hadn't been for me, and so she is alive?"

"Maybe it is as drastic as that."

"But I have no heroic memories of saving anyone from death."

Jan laughed. "It probably didn't require heroics. Maybe he went bike riding with you rather than going swimming down the valley with some other friend, at which time he would have hit his head on a rock in diving, and drowned. Or maybe he went to the candy store with you instead of to the show, and did not run out in front of that truck on the way home. There are all kinds of alternatives of which you would never have been aware."

"And I would never have had a conscious choice. It is hard to seemingly discover I had caused the death of someone."

"Just as it was a bit disturbing to learn I had caused the death of that man in the church in Centerville, what was his name?"

"George Drake."

"Yes. In all innocence I caused the events that led to his death. And in all innocence you were a necessary link in a perhaps very long string of occurrences that led to her death. Two people are alive because of *the Event*. Probably there are also many who are dead because of it, maybe even this young man who later was the source of Elizabeth's tragedy. Something obviously did happen to him to take him out of her life, though we may never find out what it was."

"Well, we'll give it a try if we can find an Annual tomorrow."

Again they drove in silence for a few blocks before John spoke again. "I think we should plan to be in Lakeland for next Sunday."

"That was the first church you had after you got out of seminary?"

"It was our first church where I was full-time and we were together. While I was appointed to Arlando you lived next to the church and I came down on weekends, but most of my time was spent at school. But at Lakeland, after two and a half years of marriage, we began to work together full-time as a team."

"John, when we leave this week–will we ever be back?"

"Oh sure, Jan. We'll come back to San Diego from time to time."

"No, I mean to live. Should we plan to do something about my things and clear out of my apartment?"

"We don't have to, but you're right. I doubt if we will ever live here again. We might do well to store what you want to keep and sell the rest, and be ready to go where we are led."

"That's what I was thinking. Then when we know where we will be living we can have it shipped to us. Those big appliances have no sentimental value for me, so we will just sell and then replace them later."

"Jan, I have been wondering something. You haven't mentioned a car and I haven't seen one. We've used the rental I picked up at the airport Tuesday. Don't you have a car?"

Jan looked across at her husband. "Don't you remember? I don't know how to drive. My parents never owned a car, so I never learned and nobody ever taught me."

Across the years John was suddenly back getting off the plane that had brought him from Oakland to San Diego on the flight home from his first year in seminary. He had come home to celebrate Christmas with his fiancée and their respective families, and then to be married on the Sunday that fell between Christmas and New Year's. He could see himself walking into the concourse at the airport and having Jan suddenly emerge from the throng of friends and relatives waiting to greet the new arrivals and throw herself into his arms.

Having kissed her with more warmth than public conduct approved, he had looked around for his parents who would, of course, be providing his transportation home or would at least have brought the car down for him to drive. But they were nowhere to be seen. Jan waited impatiently while he collected his luggage and then pulled his arm in the direction of the parking area. She led him out and across until they came to the place where his father's car was waiting.

"How did it get here?" John had asked.

"I drove it. Your dad has taught me to drive. Aren't you proud of me?" That was the occasion for a longer and even warmer kiss in place of any reply.

But that had never happened. The careful control by his father of his tendencies to be abrupt and critical in order that he might instead be gentle and patient with his future daughter-in-law... The pressure and tension of trying to learn a difficult and unfamiliar skill while pleasing and satisfying a person whose continuing good opinion of you in all things you felt to be essential... Apprehension, tension, and mutual effort growing through diligence and flowering in lasting achievement. It was now utterly gone and entirely uprooted in the obliteration of the life and influence here of Lewis A. Masters. Whatever had happened to the man he remembered as his father, he had not so much as met Jan. That easy camaraderie that father-in-law and daughter-in-law had wrought and shared until the day of his abrupt death had vanished with everything else.

"If you want to learn to drive, dearest, I shall teach you at the first opportunity."

Jan laughed. "What have I always heard about a husband teaching his wife to drive?"

"Oh, that's probably true; husbands do not do well in teaching wives this skill. But I have one great advantage; I know already what a good driver you are going to be, so I can afford to be more patient."

"Or you will remember what a good driver you knew me to be and will not really understand why it is taking me so long to achieve what you expect me to become?"

When the time finally came, it was John who was proved to be right.

THIRTY-ONE

◆

So it was then, on that Monday John returned to the Naval District to learn Washington had no record of any naval enlistment by Lewis Allen Masters. Jan and John spent the rest of the day looking through the second-hand bookstores for a copy of his High School Annual, *The Blue And White* as it was called, with the pictures, names, and remembrances of the seniors and other students at San Diego High. They had no success. Such school annuals were rarely sold to bookstores, and the few they did find were never the right year.

But the day was pleasant and it was enjoyable sharing it with each other and hoping the next musty shop they entered would give them what they sought. When they finally became convinced they would not be able to buy a copy to study at leisure, they went to San Diego High and finally found one they could examine in the school library. So in the late afternoon John sat at a table there with Jan beside him, seeking to discover persons who were inconsistent with his memories or who should have been there but now were not.

In the first category he would not be sure he found any instances at all. In the four hundred plus faces of those who had graduated with him there were some he could not personally recall and place, but this was and had always been true in a high school as large as San Diego had been at the time. The outstanding exception was, of course, the pert and delectable figure of Elizabeth Warren, the girl from down the block. Her popularity and activity in student affairs and organizations caused her to appear over and over again in the pictures of the various groups and organizations at the school. (Was that her in the picture of the Calvin Club, the on-campus Presbyterian fellowship? He could not remember whether she had been a part of it or not before, but it did surprise him.)

In the second category, John was startled to discover the only person whom he immediately missed and could not find was his own best friend, Harland Berringer. Harl had been outstanding in his scholastic achievement and in his role in student government. But each picture where he should have appeared was now complete without him.

The implications of this discovery shook John, and he redoubled his efforts to identify someone else who should have been there but was not. He tried going back in his own mind to his elementary school days and naming his friends and acquaintances in those earlier years and then seeking to remember who had continued on through junior high and high school to graduate with him, but the effort finally led nowhere.

He could not be sure any other boy was missing. He could not find a single girl in his memories who was not represented on the pages of the book before him. Given his teen-age shyness, this was what he would have expected.

He arose finally as the library began to close and walked thoughtfully down the deserted corridors beside a silent Jan. He was thinking of Elizabeth and what this might be saying about the tragedy that he remembered as happening to her. He thought back to those summer days when he and Harl had lounged on his front porch, looking across at the gleaming body absorbing as much sun as was at all proper, if not modest. They had talked about girls in general and Elizabeth in particular in ways fifteen-year-old boys do. What thoughts had persisted from those conversations? What ideas had taken root? On the day John had gone to school with the first word for his friends of the death of their prettiest classmate, he could remember no special response from Harl when he had told him as they were walking together to first period. Surprise, regret, wonder, he could remember, but no great grief or apparent guilt.

Perhaps he was jumping to conclusions. Maybe this was just coincidence and had he known where to look he would have found some linkage tying him to an older fellow, or even someone in the unexamined Junior class. Briefly he outlined to Jan his discoveries.

"Remember John, whatever it was, it now never happened. 'Like a dream, when you awaken, you despise its phantoms.'"

He kissed her lightly and they emerged into the reddening sunlight.

Then John realized the one person he had not sought here at San Diego High was he, himself. He now knew he would find nothing.

The next day, April 24th, was the last day he or Jan lived in San Diego; and it was spent in arranging to store her treasured things, selling the rest, and clearing out her apartment. It was a day of hope and hard work. Jan was clearly eager to go with her new husband into the unknown and radiated a confidence in him and in the ultimate outcome of events that he found to hard to account for in her or to duplicate in himself.

She seemed as willing to trust her welfare to his care in the future that awaited them as she was to give her body over to him in their lovemaking. It was not always easy for him to remember that, for Jan, he was still very much a strange and unknown quantity; but then he was aware that he, himself, found her subtly different than he remembered her. There was a freshness and ardor to their relationship that he felt was not entirely attributable to newness. It was as if there had been some burdens their relationship had acquired in the old life that had been shed in the new. He felt in himself he was indeed able to make her experience of being loved the goal of his own seeking; and since she could not remember a time when his reaching out to her had been self-serving and demanding rather than sensitive and loving for her, she responded with a transparent joy that multiplied his own delight and was his greatest reward.

So was their marriage being restored. Jan was still discovering new facets of her husband and of his likes and ways moment by moment, while he was in turn discovering how Jan would have been if he had given her mature love the first time, rather than having to use their relationship to discover what love should be. John had never been so happy, and his feelings were intensified in the obvious overflowing contentment of his beloved.

When in late afternoon they closed the door for the final time and turned the keys in at the manager's office, there was no sadness or nostalgia in Jan for the life that was ending here. There was instead only a great and evident eagerness for what they would find together tomorrow. John again took a room—this time a suite—in the motel where he had registered upon his arrival; and they spent their last night in the city where they were born, had met, and been married laughing and talking and planning, and being very much in love.

139

Then, early the next morning, they flew out north, to go to Lakeland.

THIRTY-TWO

◆

Shortly before three o'clock on the afternoon of Wednesday, April 25, John Masters and his wife Jan came through the mountain gap at North Pass and began the descent into the basin in which was set the large and beautiful body of water known as Skylake, at the north end of which lay the community of Lakeland. For the second time in John's experience his wife was seeing this place for the first time. Jan exclaimed over the beauties of mountains and striking blue coastline and azure sky. John silently compared the beauty that had been with the tawdriness and exploitation that had come to be since he, with Jan beside him, had first seen this place to which the bishop had sent him almost nineteen years ago. As he listened to Jan's voice and heard her excitement, he heard many of the same words and felt from her the same emotions she had uttered then.

Then they had been coming here to start together their first full-time ministry in a church they might expect to serve for more than just a dozen months or so. The preceding two years spent in the little suburban-fringe place called Arlando had been for him a part-time source of income and experience while he finished seminary. For them both it was a place to be endured until the time when, following graduation, real ministry and service could start. It was of course too bad, for the people of Arlando were no less human and needful of serious and sustained ministry than those living elsewhere, but this was the price that they paid for being a "student church" and getting their current seminarian leadership at a bargain price.

So in late June the newly ordained Reverend John L. Masters and his young wife, Jan, had come to Lakeland full of excitement and

expectation at having their first regular church to serve completely and together. They had then served here for five years—three years longer than anyone up to that time had ever stayed in what proved to be a difficult community. People who came to Lakeland tended to be those who wanted to get away from the cities and escape from the cares of modern life to the adventure of carving out for themselves a future with personal independence and success. Here, amidst the rugged mountains and beside the wildly beautiful lake, they expected to live without problems or frustrations.

In those five years both John and Jan had ministered to the disillusionment that came with the discovery that problems were not finally left behind in old places, but rather were part of the persons themselves. Sometimes the form and expression of the problem changed; but the underlying distortion of self that had made for tension and difficulties in the city or suburbs, and had made office and factory seem unbearable, was the first item packed for the move to Lakeland. It was usually unpacked and made operative while many material possessions still remained in the cartons in which they had been transported. Lakeland had no therapists, no counseling centers, and no community resources to help troubled persons come to grips with their problems. There was but one all-purpose Protestant church, and to this church a young couple had been sent to meet whatever needs there might be.

It had been an exciting five years. The hard work and the pressures derived from the problems in the lives going to pieces around them served to unify and strengthen the young marriage in the parsonage. Jan invested herself in what she saw to be her husband's ministry and accepted for herself all the things she might do "to help him." Presently she discovered she was truly experiencing a sense of "ownership" of this united ministry, so she saw she was doing not part of a task God had given John but a task that was truly hers as well. (It would be several years yet before either of them would be able to express in words the realization that when God said "husband and wife became one living being together" this meant, in a parsonage couple, they had one ministry that included them both.)

All of this John remembered.

Jan, sitting beside him, was filled still with appreciation and wonder for the beauty she was seeing. As the trees began to give way to a less regular forest of houses, John turned off on a side street and drove a few blocks to the little rustic church with the outdoor setting for summer worship. He stopped across the street and parked.

"This is it?" asked Jan. "This is where 'we served'?"

"Yep."

"For how many years?"

"Five."

"Were we happy here? I'm sure I must have been because it is so beautiful."

"We were happy to come here, happy to stay here and, finally, happy to leave."

"Isn't it funny my dreams were never of the places where we would live? As far as I know I never dreamt of anything like this or of forests or beaches or anything I have yet seen. It isn't that somehow I was glimpsing this other life we must have had together."

"No, Jan. I don't think you had those dreams out of some psychic remembrances or communication between the self you were becoming and the self that had been. I am quite sure those dreams were sent to you by God for a specific purpose."

"And that purpose was what?"

John bent over quickly and kissed her. "You fulfilled that purpose just a week ago this morning."

Jan pretended to pout: "I thought you had forgotten our 'weekiversary.' You did remember."

"Of course. How could I forget? You saved my life. Really, Jan, I was coming to the place where I knew I couldn't take any more. A week ago last night, when I saw you get out of your friend's car and go into the apartment, I almost drove away. I couldn't bear the pain of having it be your face that looked at me blankly with the 'do I know you?' expression of indifference and unconcern."

Jan laughed. "I couldn't imagine who could be coming so late at night. And then you called my name, and somehow it sounded familiar. So I looked around the safety-chained door, and it was you. The face I had seen a thousand times in those dreams that were always so real and so warm. And then, next thing I knew, you were bending over me on the couch; and I realized, finally, this was no dream."

"Do I live up to your expectations?"

"Pretty much. I guess you'll have to do."

"Maybe if you will blink several times real hard you will wake up and I will go away."

"If I need to I'll try that, but certainly not yet." She was laughing, but then she choked the laugh off. "Oh John, I do love you. I finally feel complete. It is as if this last week I have finally become who I was supposed to be."

"Then you can begin to understand what I went through when I was sure I had lost you."

Jan's long passionate kiss was answer enough, and John was surprised that her cheek touching his was wet. He sat back and watched joyful tears well up in large and beautiful eyes, then said, "Enough of this love-making. We must get to work." He opened the door and got out, hurried around the car to help Jan alight, then took her arm as they walked toward the church building.

"What are we looking for?" Jan asked.

"I really don't know. We know what we are going to find: No recollection of us, no record of anything that we ever did unless it was also done by the folks who stood in for us or followed us in the church. There will perhaps be some difference that I will notice in people and things, but it has been so long since we were here it will be hard for me to be sure how much difference I am really seeing and how much is simply normal change."

"I'm very glad to be here, dear; but I really don't know why you made the effort and spent the time when you know what you are going to find. I don't see how it is going to help."

"I don't know how to explain, Jan, except to say I feel it was important for us to come. I just expect there will be something that we will find or do that is necessary. What more can I say?"

"That's enough, husband. Your troublesome wife is satisfied. Lead on."

The front door of the church was unlocked, and they entered the apparently empty building. Much was familiar, many things were different, but all appeared to be well cared for. A chart on the wall reflecting attendance levels caught John's eye, and he examined it carefully.

Of course, having served a church a pastor kept track of its subsequent history from wherever he might currently be serving, and John had been painfully aware that after he and Jan had left this place it had fallen on hard times. There had been some good leadership, but there had also been some real mistakes in the pastors sent here, and the membership and participation in the church they had so carefully nurtured had drained away, leaving only a faithful handful attempting to keep the church open.

But this chart, showing the growth week by week of the congregation, indicated three services were now necessary each Sunday morning, and this was a thriving center for the lives of a significantly large number of people.

It was obvious to him that, because he and Jan had not been here, something had gone right. Someone had come with a different emphasis, a particular personality or approach, and had ignited a fire of fellowship and participation that was now obviously in full blaze. He thought of those faithful ones whom he knew to be still hard at work here, and how satisfying it must be to them to see their labors and dedication bear so much fruit. He was glad for them, even as he was just a bit disappointed that he had not been part of such a recipe for eventual success. He looked around and noticed some of the symbols and decorations that had been made and fastened to the walls in lieu of stained glass, which had never even been thought of in this church. He recognized in the symbols an emphasis on the Holy Spirit and His gifts, the sure signs of the Renewal movement within the church. Was this the secret of the spiritual prosperity that the chart reflected?

Jan also was looking about in appreciation. "This is really a nice little church. I feel very much at home here. I guess you would tell me I once was."

John nodded. "We did a lot together in this room. But not as much as is being done now."

"I'm sure nobody ever did a better job here than you did," Jan began, then stopped and laughed at the look on her husband's face. "Well, I just have confidence in you, dearest."

"Thank you. Nice, but not necessary. Everything is for the service and glory of God. But I would like to meet the pastor who is accomplishing so much here when there seemed to be so little promise, at least in the years after we left."

As if on cue the door to what John knew to be the stairway, leading to an office that had been carved out of attic space, opened and a figure appeared in the doorway. It wore a light blue clerical shirt with the traditional clergy collar, a darker blue skirt and pert stylish blue shoes. "Is there something I can do for you?" asked the well-modulated soprano voice.

The pastor was a more than attractive woman in her early thirties.

THIRTY-THREE

◆

"Is there something I can do for you?"

John was searching his memory for a name to go with the face and figure of the young woman who stood on the steps looking down at them. He did remember her from glimpses at annual conferences and he knew her name would be familiar when he heard it. He could not remember whether or not she was married. "I'm John Masters and this is my wife, Jan, Miss. . .

Mrs...."

She spoke quickly to settle the question: "Reverend Bernetti— Millie Bernetti— and I am not married."

"Well, Millie, we are Reverend John Masters and Jan. Some years ago we were, well, involved in helping out here for a while; and we thought we would stop by and see how things are going." This was as close to the entire truth as John felt he could comfortably come.

Millie came down the steps, obviously happy to greet a colleague. "How long ago was it you were here?"

"Back, maybe twenty-five years or so."

"That would be when Woodsen was here? Or Carper?"

John could remember a man named Woodsen who had been in the conference briefly about twenty years ago. He could not remember Carper at all. "It was Woodsen, I think, or some name like that. It was a long time ago."

"From the records that are left, not a whole lot was happening around here in those days." Millie was obviously trying to figure out how he had fitted into this struggling church in that period. She asked what she was thinking, "What did you do here?"

"Calling, mostly. Counseling. Tried to get things organized. Summer ministry to the crowds and attempting to get something going for the young people. We were sent here to try to make things go better, and did what we could."

All true, so far as it went. Of course, in terms of the past of this church now, they had never been here and had accomplished precisely nothing.

"I did preach in the outdoor chapel out there. We used to move the organ out and store it in a little shed in those days for the summer crowds."

Millie brightened. "Oh yes, I have heard them talk about doing that years ago. The organ's permanently installed in here now, though we do risk a piano from the Sunday school when July comes. But those summer crowds no longer impress us with their size."

"No, I guess not." John followed her gaze to the attendance charts. "This place seems to be taking off, with three services each Sunday morning during what used to be the quiet season."

Millie's hands moved unconsciously to smooth her skirt. "Yes, it surely has. Praise God. It wasn't like this when I came here three years ago."

"So you are responsible for all this?"

"God is responsible for it. John, I came here three years ago fresh from Hilltop Theological Seminary as a Christian and a minister, but with no precise idea of what the Gospel was really about. I knew a lot of things about the Old and New Testaments and had taken a lot of classes in preaching and church history and administration and counseling and all the rest; but I also had a lot to learn. I came up here to try to breathe life into a congregation that had been struggling for years without ever getting anywhere. They had never had more than fifty members in their entire experience, and it seemed possible the church would just fade away and die altogether. My predecessor had quit the ministry and cleared out early in the year, and when I came there had been no pastor for nine months."

"No one had been supplying?"

"Nope. Week by week the few remaining faithful ones came together and fashioned their own worship. If it hadn't been for Molly and Cliff, I just don't know what would have happened."

"Molly and Cliff? I don't remember. . ."

"No, I don't think they were here when you would have been

around. They aren't here now. But at that time a new highway was being built and Cliff Burrows had come up to work on it—he is a heavy equipment operator—and they came to this church just when it needed them. They want to be helpful and supportive, and they love the Lord. Oh, how they love the Lord."

"They kept things going?"

"There was a leadership vacuum and they just drifted in and quietly filled it. Cliff played the guitar and they both sang, and they would take turns sharing and talking about what they had learned from the Scriptures. And they had a ministry of healing. So, when I got here I found a solid nucleus of Christians who had been faithful to their church for years and now saw first-hand what the church could be. When folks came with needs, especially for healing, Cliff would pray. And he got results. I appeared on the scene and everybody looked at me fearfully as if I was going to come in and spoil what they had just been discovering. No former minister had ever talked to them about the presence and power of Jesus in a way they could really believe and see, and they were afraid I would not like what was going on or understand what the Burrows had been doing."

John grinned. "Well, did you?"

Millie laughed. "Not at first. Seminary hadn't prepared me for this. But Molly and Cliff came and talked to me in such a loving way. They made it plain they wanted me to be their pastor and they were submitting to my authority. They would do nothing I didn't completely approve of. The kind of things they talked about as having happened sounded like they were right out of the Book of Acts. I had been taught to think of such things as stories made up by the early church to illustrate what they thought the power of God could have done to validate the mission and authority of the Apostles. But Molly and Cliff were so gentle and so sure, and I couldn't tell them they couldn't do what they had been doing. So I told them I would watch and see before I made any decisions. And so I did."

"And what did you see?" This was Jan's question, with just a glance at her husband.

"What I never expected to see. Miracles. People healed. Marriages restored. Lives changed. In the first service on Sunday after I arrived, we had just finished the first hymn and I was ready to begin my opening prayer when Lucy Parmentier stood up and asked if we could pray for the healing of a friend she had brought with her that morning. The woman had a couple of crushed disks in her back and was in constant pain. The doctors had told her she was a candidate for spinal fusion, if and when she could come up with the money. But that would not be possible for some time the way things were, and she was desperate for relief. I don't know what I would have done if Cliff had not stood up and asked for permission from me (in that great way he has) to pray with me for the healing."

"The next thing I knew someone had put a chair in the middle of the platform and the woman was being helped forward. Then Cliff came up, along with Molly and some of the others. He set her in the chair, put my hands on her head, and then put his hands beside mine. The others laid their hands on our shoulders and Cliff began to pray. He spoke very quietly and his prayer was full of praise and confidence. He just believed Jesus was there and wanted to heal, and he seemed to be so full of joy he could not speak without kind of chuckling quietly to himself and to the Lord. But I felt power. I can't describe to you quite how I knew but there was something, a bright clean warm power flowing into that woman's body. After several minutes Cliff stopped and kind of nudged me as if to indicate it was time now for the pastor to pray—and necessary. So I muttered a few words of thanks to God for what He had begun to do, and I closed with 'in Jesus' Name, Amen.' And that woman got up well. If I hadn't seen it with my own eyes I wouldn't have believed it. She was so amazed and delighted she was crying with joy and relief and surprise."

"And it was not just a temporary thing—some induced release of body chemicals that stopped the pain temporarily?"

"The woman was healed. That was almost four years ago and she is just fine. Her doctor is also my doctor, and I have asked him about her. He just shakes his head. He has no explanation for how her back was restored to its original condition."

"And the service—your first service in this church—went on from there as if nothing had happened?"

"Oh, let me tell you I felt my sermon was a terrible disappointment to anyone who had seen what we had seen. But they were polite and loving, and my sermons began to change. I began to read the New Testament with a new expectation, and I found myself seeing Jesus and hearing His words with a freshness and a wonder I had never felt before."

"I began to really notice all of the promises Jesus makes to us about

His presence and His power through prayer and the church, if we will only believe and expect and obey. My sermons began to change and people began to tell me how really glad they were I had come. With the beginning of the summer season, I had been told, the tourists would come in great numbers but the locals would drop off, having too much work to do to be in church. But they came and asked for a service at nine o'clock on Sunday night, so they wouldn't be away from the Lord and His body. It was just great. And I noticed more and more people were being brought to church and introduced to me. The word was spreading that there was good news at our church, and more and more people began to come to hear it."

John nodded and smiled. "So you and this Burrows couple are a kind of ministry team?"

"Not now. Within a year the Burrows had moved on to another job down state, but God raised up others to take their places and the ministry goes on and grows. Day by day we are having more ex-alcoholics and ex-gamblers find the purpose for which God made them, and we see them go with power to bring their families and friends into the church that has made such a difference in their lives."

Millie suddenly looked at her watch. "Oh, I'm sorry but I'm late now for an appointment. If you're going to be here, why don't you come back tonight at eight for the prayer fellowship that meets here? This will show you better than I can tell it what is happening here these days. Can you?"

John nodded.

"Good. Sorry I have to run," and in a swirl of very feminine movements she was gone.

John looked at his wife. She was very thoughtful. It occurred to him there was a lot about himself he had not yet shared with her.

THIRTY-FOUR

◆

A few minutes before eight that evening, Jan and John returned to the church. Folding chairs had been arranged in a circle, and upwards of two dozen people were already sitting, standing, talking, and laughing around the room. Four or five of them were familiar to John from his remembered years here, and he thought perhaps another five might have recognizable names from having been in the area though uninvolved with the church in those days. The rest were newcomers to Skylake as might be expected in such a transient area. But they were clearly familiar and well-known to each other, as they laughed and shared and greeted new arrivals with good humor and apparent love.

Millie Bernetti was no longer garbed in the uniform of her calling but was wearing a muted and very feminine pastel dress that made her look pretty and appealing. John looked about at the make-up of the group. Acknowledging that men were attracted to the Christian fellowship when it is manifesting vitality and power and the sensible real presence of Jesus Christ, still one had to wonder if there were not some of this majority of men who attended in hopes of deepening a relationship with a most alluring pastor.

Millie came at once to greet them on their arrival and, being reminded again of their first names, introduced John and Jan to two other couples and left them in their charge. John found it expedient to be vague in answering questions about residence and current employment, for they were not so far from Centerville as to be sure someone present might not know the church and pastor. So John affirmed his clergy status but left questions about where he was currently serving unanswered under the cover of being "between churches at the moment."

Jan remained silent and smiling and John could not help noticing that, as usual, almost every male eye in the room took opportunity to look at her and linger there for as long as was practical without being too noticeable. This was always the effect Jan's loveliness had, and John had become used to it across the years. Jan never gave any sign she noticed, although of course she did. But John could feel in this Jan a tension and uncertainty of what to expect that went with the newness of a group and situation, like this was to her.

Before the Event, Jan had been familiar with such prayer groups and found her place in them easily and gracefully. She had matured in the awakening of the Holy Spirit as it had come to be experienced around them in the two decades when she and John had served in their churches. It had been a discovery and a development that they had shared and grown in together.

But now Jan was making an abrupt transition between the church into which she had been born, formal and structured and asleep, and the church as it was coming to be—alive, powerful, and abounding in miracles. She was clearly unsure of what was to be expected, either of the evening or of her.

A spate of latecomers had entered the room and John caught a look and a nod from Millie to a man standing beside his wife at a point furthest from the door in the growing and irregular circle of chairs. Being thus signaled he spoke, "Okay, I guess it's time for us to get started. Will you all find seats and settle down."

The crowd quickly assorted itself and became settled in the oval, and John noticed a single chair had appeared in the center to be left unoccupied. Under the eye and smiling face of the leader, silence fitfully descended.

"I notice we have several newcomers tonight. Would you please stand and introduce yourselves to us, beginning here on my right and going around?"

There were seven persons who now stood up. Four of them were previously unreached locals residing in Lakeland or its environs, while John and Jan and one other were transients who had heard of the meeting and had come to take part for just this evening.

The necessary amenities having been cared for, the leader looked down the circle to his pastor. "Mil, would you begin the evening for us?"

She responded by asking with a gesture for all to stand. Then she raised her hands, turned her face upward and, closing her eyes, began to pray in a clear soprano that, without being loud, was audible to everyone. She claimed the promised presence of Jesus in their midst and committed them to the doing of His will this night. "Pour out Your Holy Spirit upon us, and equip us with those gifts that will be needed to do the work of Your love in our bodies and minds and spirits, that Your Name will be glorified. Cause this night to be remembered for all eternity as a time when lives were changed and Your whole will was done by us and through us and in us. In Your Name, Lord Jesus, we pray."

"Amen, Amen, Amen." came the general response.

Now the leader called for any words of testimony or praise that might be forthcoming. Suddenly it seemed as if at least half the group had something to share of what God had done in their lives and in response to their prayers in just the week past. Guidance and healings and crucial insights were seemingly the order of the day in the experience of these people. A child whose fever vanished at a father's faithful prayer. A wayward son who had unexpectedly and contritely returned home after dad and mom had agreed in prayer they could do no more, and his rebelliousness could only be entrusted to Jesus. A business deal that seemed to be taking an unethical turn and had created doubts, but that had been contracted and now must be followed to whatever conclusion would be forthcoming—but, when prayed about, was suddenly and inexplicably renounced and called off by the only person able to do so. Lost treasures found. Misunderstandings healed. Marriages, once shaky, still further strengthened by new insights and greater awareness of love. On and on the account of the works of grace unfolded, until it seemed as if there might be a whole evening spent in telling of what had been.

At the account of each victory, each act of goodness, the group responded with exclamations of praise and thankfulness in which all were clearly rejoicing with real love and involvement in the loving kindness of God. "Thank you, Lord. Praise you, Jesus" was said often and repeatedly in response to each new word of divine care. One got the feeling it was as much a blessing to hear of the benefactions of others as it was to be personally touched. This group rejoiced in each victory personally.

But then the leader asked for what was now needed; who had requests for prayer that might be lifted to God? Again this evoked widespread participation. Friends, neighbors, co-workers were lifted up for various kinds of blessing, healing, forgiveness, guidance, and strengthening. As each need was held up, there was a time of prayer where short, fervent prayers would be spoken by two or three persons in turn, to the vocal affirmation of the rest, who made the petitions their own property before God by exclamations of approval and praise.

At length a momentary silence fell on the group, and in that pause a woman got up and made her way to the chair still unoccupied in the center of the circle. Her eyes brimmed with tears and her face worked with emotion. John recognized her as one of those who had introduced themselves as resident newcomers at the beginning of the evening. She struggled to get control of herself and then spoke: "I... I need help and I am scared. I found a lump in my breast and I, well, I put off doing anything about it. I tried to pretend it wasn't there. Now it has gotten bigger and, here are several other lumps, and I am so afraid. O God, help me." And with that she broke down and began to weep openly.

Nobody was embarrassed. Their looks showed understanding and love. The leader looked around to see whether someone was being led to pray for her. At that moment John knew who it was to be. He felt in himself that unmistakable leading of the Spirit of God which he had known occasionally for some years but had become so much more pronounced in the past three weeks. He got up and walked forward. Millie and another woman joined him, and then one by one the rest gathered behind them, laying their hands upon each other in a progressive chain that reached to where John and his first two co-workers in prayer stood beside the seated and anguished woman. John placed his hand upon her head and the others likewise touched shoulder and neck. For a moment there was silence in prayer, and then John spoke.

"Holy Spirit of God, it is Your will that this sister should be healed. Your healing power is being poured into her, and the healing and creative Light of Jesus is now beginning to work in each cell of her body, remaking them according to the purpose and plan of His wholeness. We thank you, Lord Jesus, for the power You are sending." Even as he spoke, he felt the warmth rush through his hands and rise in her head. He felt her sobbing cease as she also became aware of power at work in her body. Her hands suddenly flew to her breasts and began to probe through her clothing for sensation.

"It's gone. They're gone. Praise be to God."

John smiled. "At least they are going and will soon be gone."

"No, they really are gone. I have been so frightened. I know exactly where they are–were– and they were here just before I came up, and now they are not here. I felt such peace, such love, and such warmth, and I know I am well. Thank you, Jesus." She arose and threw her arms around John and kissed him.

"Praise God from Whom all blessing flow," John's voice began, and all the others joined in at once.

"Praise Him all creatures here below,
Praise Him above ye heavenly host,
Praise Father, Son, and Holy Ghost,
Amen. Thank you, Lord. Glory to God."

The newly healed one was scattering tears of joy as she moved about the circle, inviting the women to touch her where she had been diseased and to feel for themselves there was nothing there but what was smooth and healthy.

Someone looked at John and proclaimed in a loud voice, "It's good to have a healer in our midst tonight."

John laughed. "He's always here. Jesus is the only healer. We are just lucky enough to have Him willing to use us."

"Amen. That's right. Thank you, Lord," came the chorus of responses. The one who had initiated the remark nodded approvingly.

Millie stepped forward and looked around. "The Spirit is telling me someone here wants to be baptized with the Holy Spirit, someone special." Her eyes swept the room.

Beside him John felt movement and saw Jan walk forward. "Yes, I do.... . I've been a church member most of my life and I thought I knew all there was to know about Christ, but it is apparent I have a lot to learn. Whatever He has for me, I want."

Millie gestured for her to be seated in the chair, and looked across at John. He smiled and nodded his answer to the question her eyes were asking.

Quickly the group gathered around, laying their hands upon Jan, or upon those who stood in front of them where they could not crowd within arms length of her seated form.

Millie spoke quietly. "Jan, Jesus came to baptize us not with water but with the Holy Spirit of God, equipping us with God's power that we might obey and serve Him in doing God's work. Are you wholly committed to obeying Jesus Christ in all things and doing His Holy

Will?"

"I am."

"Lord Jesus, pour out upon Jan your servant the fullness of The Spirit. Clothe her with power from On High. Grant to her Your purposes and Your ministry, and give her such gifts of The Holy Spirit as she may use with profit or need from time to time to glorify Your Name and do Your holy will. Thank you, Jesus. Amen."

The group was beginning to make its way back to their seats when a strong voice spoke out of their midst: "John, My child, know that you are precious in My sight. You do not understand what has happened to you, but it is enough for you to know you are in my care. I have held your life in My hand, and I have preserved you from a harm you could not comprehend. You are obeying My word, and I am pleased with your obedience. In this place you are seeking, and in this place you will find what will make the truth known to you. Continue to trust and to praise, and My love will be made known in all things, even better than before."

The voice ceased and there was again a general chorus of thanks and praise to Christ for the prophecy that had come.

John listened with particular care to every word. For the voice by which that prophecy had come had been Jan's, his wife.

THIRTY-FIVE

♦

John awoke before dawn and knew he would sleep no more. Quietly he slipped from beside his wife out of the bed and put on clothes and shoes sufficient for walking in the early morning calm. Making sure he had the key, he slipped out the door, locking it behind him for his sleeping wife.

He turned toward the lakefront and the beach that ran for a mile or more at this part of the lake. The sun had not yet risen over the mountains that rimmed the far side of the lake, but the predawn light was sufficient to walk by. Skylake itself was covered with a thick mist rising from the relatively warmer waters into the cold mountain air. Little could be seen of the lake surface.

John turned left as he approached the water's edge and walked northward beside the still gray water. He thought of the prayer group last night and the wonder and joy that had come to Jan as a result. He acknowledged to himself what he had not admitted to Jan: surprise that she had prophesied. This had never been an experience she had "before." When she had then become aware of her gift it had been that of organization and administration, a gift sorely needed in their united ministry. He had no doubt she would also bring this gift to their life together again. Perhaps what had taken place last night was merely a manifestation gift, a temporary and one-time action of the Holy Spirit to make known His Presence in her by giving a needed word through her. Yes, that was possible and indeed there was no sure way for him to know at this moment; somehow, he did not feel this was the case. He suspected from now on they would be blessed with having her as a prophet, a channel for God's word relevant to persons and situations—a very great and important gift indeed.

And what of himself? Before the Event he had the ministry gift of being a pastor-teacher. It was true that on several occasions over the years he had been given a manifestation of the gift of healing, but with nothing like the regularity and impact of the past four weeks. Last night someone had talked about him as a "healer" and he knew how important such group-given discernment could be. It seemed this might be also a new ministry gift for him.

He thought of last night's group, and of the other five such that Millie told him took place in scattered times during the week. Several were as large as that one had been, while others were smaller and more specialized. A men's group met early for breakfast on Mondays, while a group of young people shared together in the power and love of God on Saturday nights. John could see now where the power was coming from to transform the struggling church he had known here into this thriving fellowship rivaling in attendance the largest churches in this district.

All of this, because he had not taken his place in the cavalcade of events in the life of this community. Not because he was in those beginning days of his ministry a bad pastor; indeed, perhaps it was his efficiency and the results of his partial success that had kept this from happening in the world he had known. This church had never seen him now, and it had never grown to the deceptive size he had coaxed out of these people in the five years he spent here. They had remained smaller and struggled harder. The conference-assigned leadership had been less qualified and had culminated in one man leaving the church to its own devices. Out of this, God had caused to grow one of His great victories.

The first bright rays of the sun were now hitting the tops of the pines and cedars growing up to the edge of the beach. Suddenly the sullen silver world was gilded with brightest gold. John turned and looked at the golden haze that lay on the bosom of the lake and, he knew, now would shortly disappear. This place was still beautiful, even if it was not as pristine and unspoiled as it had been when he had first known it. Those had been good times. But these were better. According to every value he held dear, things now in this place were more promising and more fruitful than they had ever been before. He stood quietly, drinking in beauty.

He glanced at his watch. He had been out for more than half an hour. It would soon be time for them to have breakfast and decide the directions and goals for the day. He turned and began to retrace his steps toward the resort motel where they had spent the night. This was the most beautiful time of the day for him here, as it had always been, and he deliberately soaked up all the sights and sounds and feelings against that moment when he must again leave this beauty behind and hold it only in memory.

Some slight sound from out on the lake caught his attention In the mists something was stirring. He peered into the golden glare. At first he could make nothing out, but then a part of the haze seemed to solidify into the vague shadow of a boat and a man rowing toward the pier jutting out from the end of the motel that was his own destination. As he drew near, the man came rowing out of the fog and up to the near side of the jetty.

"Good mornin'."

"Good morning," John replied. "How was the fishing?"

The man placed tackle box and pole on the pier surface and prepared to stand and step out of his now secured boat. "Disappointin'. Not at all what I hoped for, but I guess I'm trying to recapture my childhood. Had an uncle who lived at Wolcott, on Lake Ontario. When I'd go to visit him we'd often go out to fish on the lake just before dawn. My memories of those days are of the best fishin' I ever had. Thought maybe it would be the same here, but it sure didn't work out."

Something jogged John's childhood memories. "Wolcott—isn't that in western New York State?"

"Yeah. I was born and raised in Lymanville. Little place, maybe seven, eight hundred people when I left."

"Ever hear of a place called Ridgeham?"

"Oh sure, about five miles away across the fields. A bit more by road if you're driving."

John looked carefully at the man. *Must be sixty or sixty-five years old*, he estimated to himself. *Old enough to maybe know something about my family.*

"Did you ever know a family in Ridgeham named Masters?"

The man smiled. "Sure. Leastways, my dad did. Knew Allen Masters and his wife June real well. I can remember spending a lot of time playing around that old house as a kid while the folks were inside talkin'. Great family."

"Yeah. Well, my name is John Masters."

"You a relative of theirs?"

"Grandson. My dad was Lewis Masters." John waited to see what would happen.

"Lewis' son. Well, this is a small world. So Lewis made somethin' of himself after all. You know, I have to tell you my folks never thought much of your dad, doing what he did."

"What was that?"

"Oh, runnin' away and never lettin' 'em know what had become of him. Back about the time I was born he took off one night. Left a note sayin' goodbye, and that was the last they ever heard of him. Never a hint again as long as they lived whether he was alive or dead. They sure never heard anythin' of you. It was as if he had just up and vanished off the face of the earth."

Suddenly John was back home in the familiar front room at San Diego. In his memory he could see his father sitting opposite him, telling him about his own teen-age years. "John, I got to hating and misunderstanding my father and mother so much that, when I was eighteen, I ran away. One night when they were in bed asleep I pinned a note to my pillow, took a few things and what money I had and struck out for myself. Managed to make my way to Rochester and the next day joined the Navy. I didn't get back to see them for almost six years, although by then I had written my apologies and everything was long since smoothed over. And by then I knew why my dad had been so strict with me, and what he was trying to do for me the best way he knew how." And he had then gone on to talk about how he would also try to do what was best for John, even if it did not always dovetail with what John wanted or expected.

John's thoughts returned to the present.

"He never wrote? Are you sure?"

"Not a word. Ever. I guess I am a bit relieved myself to know the story turned out so well. What do you do?"

"I am a United Connectional pastor."

The other laughed. "That's sure a turn. Whatever might of been said about the Masters family I knew, religion was not their strong suit."

"From what I have heard I'm sure you are right. But things change."

"They sure do, and this has been a good morning for me, just meetin' you. Have you ever been back to Ridgeham?"

"Never have. Have I missed much?"

"Nothin' really to see, 'cept maybe the blast site. That is interestin'.'"

"Blast site?"

"Sure, you've read about it. You must have. 'The famous New York State Mystery Explosion'—mentioned most often as a possible little cousin of that Siberian Meteorite explosion of 1908, 'cept no one saw it fall. It used to be written up a lot in Sunday Supplements."

John had always had a special interest in such things. He had never read of any such blast in western upstate New York, or any place nearby. He was familiar in detail with the Siberian explosion, but he could remember no recent occurrence in the New World that was ever compared to it. "Funny, I just don't seem to remember it. What happened?"

"One night just before I was born there was a sudden big explosion about two miles out of town between Ridgeham and Lymanville. Whatever it was hit in a wooded area and blew a hole in the ground and the explosion leveled a clearin' about fifty yards long and maybe thirty wide. As a kid my dad would take folks who were visitin' us from elsewhere out to the spot and tell 'em of the broken windows and the bright flash that woke them all up that night. I remember lookin' it up when I got to high school and I found it wasn't as late as he had always let on, just a few minutes after eight when the explosion came."

"What caused it?"

"Nobody ever figured that out. They dug around a lot and probed deep into the ground, but far as I know nobody never found anythin'. It was just a big bang that made a funny hole in the ground."

"Nobody was near enough to see it?"

"Nope. No one was anywheres near, and as they say, 'there were no casualties.' Just a place for crowds of people to come and look, for a while. They were still comin' when I was a kid, and I guess some scientists and professors still come sometimes, tryin' to figure out what it was happened."

Suddenly John saw in his mind's eye the map in his suitcase, the airline route map with the penciled notes and line reaching out across the country from the West Coast back across space and time to end exactly over the place where Ridgeham was located. "And all this happened in February, about sixty-five years ago?"

"Did I say February? But you know, I think you're right. It was several months before I was born, and it seems to me it was February.

162

But how did you know?"

"Maybe my dad did tell me about it after all."

"Could be. It was about the time he left, I think."

The coincidence was growing into an appalling possibility. And how much of a coincidence was it to meet this man from the Ridgeham area on this beach this morning? (Could Christians believe in coincidence?)

"So long, Reverend Masters. I can't tell you how happy I am to have met you. I've got to be in San Francisco for a doctor's appointment at eleven-thirty, so I'd best be on my way. I hope someday you get to Ridgeham." He picked up his tackle, strode around the corner and was gone.

"In this place you are seeking, and in this place you will find what will make the truth known to you." Thus Jan had spoken through the Spirit last night.

He knew where they had to go today.

Within an hour he and Jan packed the car, checked out of the motel and headed for Reno and breakfast at the airport there.

Shortly after nine o'clock a car drew up in front of the motel, near the unit so recently vacated by John and Jan. A man in a dark suit got out and strode into the office.

"I'm looking for a Reverend John Masters. Can you tell me where I might find him?"

The manager looked up and shrugged. "I'm sorry but they checked out the better part of two hours ago."

"Do you know where they were going?"

"I really didn't hear them say. They headed up the hill toward Nevada when they pulled out."

"Could you give me an address where I might find them?"

"They didn't leave any forwarding address with me."

"But surely he had to give you a permanent address on his registration?" The stranger watched the eye movements of the man behind the desk and was not disappointed.

"I'm sorry. We are not allowed to give out that information."

"It's important to me and I will make it worth your while to help me out." He pulled out his wallet.

"I think you'd better be going now, mister. We have no more to say to each other."

The suited man started to say something else, but thought better of

163

it, turned on his heel, snatched one of the business cards in the container on the counter and strode out the door. He walked briskly to his car and drove away in a swirl of dust and a spatter of gravel.

The car slowed and stopped a few yards beyond the end of the motel buildings, where the driver took out and opened a cell phone and dialed the number from the card he had just obtained.

In the motel office the manager was again busying himself with routine work when the phone rang. He picked it up, listened for a moment, and then bolted for the lakeside units on a dead run.

Again, the car bearing the inquisitive suited stranger backed recklessly up and stopped in front of the office. Quickly the man dodged inside and leafed hurriedly through the file of recent registration cards that the manager's glance had earlier identified for him. It was the work of but a few seconds to find the card headed "Reverend John L. Masters (2)" and remove it from the file. He was out the door again and driving away before the manager could discover the person calling for help so urgently from Unit 32 did not in fact exist and would begin to wonder why a senseless joke had been pulled so early in the season on this morning.

THIRTY-SIX

◆

Friday morning, April 27th.

Again John awakened before dawn.

The motel room clock showed the time to be five twenty-eight and it took him a few moments to remember where he was. Yesterday had been a day of travel; from Lakeland to Reno by car, then from Reno to Chicago by air, followed by a shorter flight from Chicago to Buffalo, New York. Then they had rented a car and driven east and north to Orion, the seat of Lakeside County where Ridgeham was located. They had arrived after dark last night, too late to do anything but find this motel and walk for a few blocks together through the warm spring night.

This was new country for John. It might have been familiar territory for his father and home for generations of his forebears, but John had never before been here. His grandfather Masters had died before his birth and his grandmother had lived on alone, for him a distant reality from whom he had received cards and presents at Christmas and on birthdays up through his early teens. San Diego was a continent away from this quiet corner of New York and it was a distance his family had been unable to transcend. There was no question about what he remembered: Lewis, his father, had made himself known to his family and been reconciled to them, but no visit by either mother or son to the other was ever contemplated as more than a possibility that might someday be undertaken. It never happened. Nor had his uncle or aunt or their families been more than occasionally mentioned abstractions that had no real part in his day-to-day life.

How John now wished he might have listened more carefully to his father's recollections of his life. He might then have had the impulse to ask questions about precise places and dates. He never had. He could remember his dad had left home—"run away" according to his own description, though at eighteen it was perhaps not a proper term—and immediately joined the Navy. His "boot camp" was at the Great Lakes Naval Training Station. Then he had been assigned to duty in Norfolk, Virginia and had gone to sea from there.

The ship to which he was initially assigned had then been shifted to the Pacific Fleet on the West Coast. Were there stories told in childhood about the brief stay in Norfolk? If there were, he could not remember them. His dad had first arrived in San Diego a year after joining the service and for a time he was stationed there. Then it had been off to the Far East. Beyond that, he knew his dad had served on destroyers and had gone home on leave to Ridgeham, six years after he had left, for a reunion with the family.

What would he find this morning? In his planned stops at the County Clerk's office and the Lakeview Register newspaper office, what could he expect to find? He must not expect too much.

He lay back flat against the bed looking straight up at the ceiling, closed his eyes and addressed himself in prayer to God. He spoke praise in his heart for all that had been given to him in recent days, especially the blessing of Jan and how happy she had seemed to be, ever since the prayer meeting night before last. Once again John felt the divine Presence answer him in the form of deep and abiding awareness of peace and well-being:

It's all right. Trust.

John let the feeling fill him and roll over him. He luxuriated in it.

Then the sun was streaming in the window and it was eight-thirty. Jan was leaning over him, smiling and saying, "Come on, sleepy head, wake up."

So breakfast was late, and they did not arrive at the county clerk's office until shortly after ten. John made inquiries about the routine to be followed in getting access to old records, and began the search. It was quickly established: Lewis Allen Masters, son of Allen R. Masters and June Windham Masters, was born on December 5 some eighty-four years ago, with a doctor in attendance, at home in Ridgeham, New York. Beyond that there was no record that referred to him, until John thought to ask for the file on the will of Allen and then of June. Allen's will, filed for probate almost exactly fifty years ago, on June 27th, simply gave all goods and property to his beloved wife, June. But her will, filed subsequent to her death fourteen years later gave her estate in equal parts to a son, Howard, and a daughter, Alice—"since my other son, Lewis Allen Masters has been for these many years absent and unaccounted for and must be presumed dead. Should the aforesaid Lewis Allen Masters make himself known and present himself at or after the time of my death, he shall inherit from this estate, as his entire share and inheritance, the sum of One Dollar ($1.00) to be paid him out of the distribution."

It was clear then that *the Event* had prevented his father from accomplishing the reconciliation John remembered as having happened.

Nothing further was discovered amidst the official records.

By the time they emerged from the County Clerk's Office it was already well past noon. Breakfast was still too recent to permit concern about food, but Jan and John did stop for a cup of coffee before tackling the office of the weekly newspaper. Here it took some talking for John to persuade the editor to let him look through the yellowing back files of the publication.

He began his search with the account of the local high school graduation for Ridgeham High in the year when his father graduated. The edition of the Lakeview Register for Friday, June 13, (the paper was published every Friday in those days) listed the graduating class and described the ceremonies of graduation. No other mention was made of Lewis A. Masters than to list him as one of those receiving his diploma. He was therefore amongst those who were "warmly congratulated" by the editor upon the "successful completion of their long years of diligent study."

A careful scanning of the editions in the following weeks turned up no further mention of Lewis or anyone else in the Masters clan. The next item of interest completely occupied the first page of the edition of Friday, February 20, in the following year. "MYSTERY EXPLOSION NEAR RIDGEHAM" the headline proclaimed. John read with growing interest that first hurried account.

Wednesday night about twelve minutes after eight the peace of our verdant countryside was disrupted by a violent upheaval that shattered windows in Ridgeham and Lymanville and was heard as far away as Rochester, Buffalo, and even in Toronto. Several of our subscribers were outside and saw the brilliant flash that lighted up the heavens brighter than a hundred lightening bolts, but no one to whom your correspondent has yet talked can give any hint of having seen anything before the blast. Wally Hamford was looking right at the blast when it occurred and was blinded for some minutes by its brilliance, he reports.

The blast happened about a mile and a quarter east-northeast of Ridgeham in a stand of trees belonging to the Harrington Place. The actual site of the blast includes a stretch of the spur track belonging to the New York Central Railroad.

Upon examination, your correspondent found the blast to have been of unusual intensity, beyond anything he or anyone with whom he has talked has ever seen. The blast took place in the center of an oval crater of destruction about fifty yards long by perhaps forty yards wide. Around this area many trees have been uprooted and blown down by the force of the blast. In the center is a depression, perhaps eight to ten inches below the former level of the ground, that has been fused by the heat and force of the explosion into a glass-like basin your reporter measured to be fifty-six feet long and thirty-four and a half feet wide at the greatest extent. Into this basin at one point the rails on one side of the right-of-way for the railroad vanish. The rest of the roadbed nearby has been so twisted and torn up it will require much work by the railroad crew to restore service.

It has been suggested this was the work of anarchists attempting to strike at society by blowing up the railroad, but the explosion centered well away from the right of way, and no one with whom it was possible to speak could begin to say what explosive could have created such a result. The mystery was deepened by the evidence of unusually intense heat that scarred the area in ways beyond the experience of anyone who has yet visited the site. It is understood that scientists from the University of Rochester will be there today, so perhaps we will be able to give some definite word on the cause of this occurrence in our next edition. Let us rejoice that the damage was confined to windows, remote woodlands, and a railroad track then empty of traffic, and there was none of the loss of life and property that could have been so widespread if this had happened closer to some center of population.

John leafed quickly to the next issue, the one for the 27th of February. Again the mystery took the lion's share of page one and spilled over into other parts of the paper. The coming of the promised academic experts had seemingly done nothing to dispel the questions regarding the nature and origin of the explosion. The idea had been raised of a possible meteorite fall, but this had been just as promptly discounted because there were several persons who had been outside and looking in the right direction who did not report seeing any streak of light descending to the point of the explosion, including a very definite and highly articulate Wally Hamford. One strange item was alluded to almost parenthetically, the dogs of the area began howling after the explosion. It developed there had come to be an unrest bordering on frenzy in the canine community, and this had begun suddenly after the thing had happened. This too was wondered at and complained about, but not explained.

An item that did gather a great deal of attention in the whole affair was the total ruination of all photographic film in the neighborhood; and the seeming inability of photographers from outside the area to come away from their visit to the explosion site with any usable pictures of it. Packages of photographic film on drugstore shelves and in cameras would appear to be perfectly fine until processed, when it was discovered they had been entirely and completely fogged to the obliteration of any recorded images. (This was in fact only gradually realized as there were few photographers in the region who took enough pictures to make the discovery right away.) But the scientists who came and attempted to record what they were seeing found upon return to their academic darkrooms that their film was also completely black and retained no images whatsoever.

John read on, week by week. The explosive was unidentified, the source of the explosion still undefined. More and more scientists were asserting this was, in fact, an unusual meteoric phenomenon and those who had claimed to be in a position to see it were in fact not looking where they had claimed to be, and had anyone truly been sighting toward the East and a little north at 8:13 P.M. on the night of the 18th of February last they must have seen a bright trail that would have terminated without a doubt in that explosion. To which the locals replied sullenly they knew what they had not seen, or words to that effect.

Finally a woman from the village of Lymanville, beyond the explosion site, came forward to describe in gratifying detail having seen a bright streak in the heavens that came down right where the bright flash of the explosion followed for her admiring and awestruck gaze. She was the celebrity of the hour, as far as the visiting professors were concerned, though there was a hint that her neighbors did not regard her as brimming over with reliability, and the question began to fade. The tracks were repaired, the meteorite was probed for, and the crowds going to the place began to decline. And, at last, the dogs stopped howling as suddenly as they had begun.

Ultimately the whole story vanished from the papers altogether. John hurried on through the files. He stopped again to read carefully the edition of Friday, June 28, a decade later. There was a proper and appreciative obituary for Allen R. Masters, aged sixty-two, who had died suddenly of a heart attack in his home the morning before, and whose services would be held on Monday at the local funeral home. Survived by his wife, June, and his son Howard and daughter Alice, he had also been the father of Lewis A. Masters who had disappeared some years before and was presumed dead. Finally John came to the edition for the 24th of September, thirty-six years ago, to find the notice of the death and impending burial of June Masters at the age of seventy-four, from a stroke. Again there was the listing of surviving children (still Alice and Howard) and this time the grandchildren, but now there was no mention of the lost if not forgotten Lewis.

John leafed on through the file copies aimlessly. He found a note where a local young would-be Uranium prospector had taken a Geiger counter out to the site of the presumed meteorite fall and found there was, indeed, a slightly higher radiation count in the area than in the surrounding ground. He reported having written this fact to the authorities at the University, but whatever their answer to him might have been did not subsequently appear in print.

John looked up and was surprised at the lateness of the hour and the redness of the sun slanting through the window. Jan sat patiently beside him looking over his shoulder. He was sure now that this explosion had something to do with the Invisible Radiating Anomaly discovered over California by the evidence of its x-rays. To his mind this was confirmed by the time and place of the explosion on the crude curve that he had constructed on the map. The strange behavior of the dogs after the explosion might well be related to the launching of this object and its still being close enough to the ground for some high-pitched sound to be of sufficient intensity to disturb the tender ears of household pets. But what was it and how did this impinge on the life of Lewis Allen Masters, eighteen and a half, and about to seek in the wider world for his own fortune and future?

His reverie was interrupted by word the office was closing and it would be necessary for them to leave. John stopped by the desk and placed and paid for a year's subscription to be sent to him at St. Matthew's Church in Denver, and then he and Jan walked out into the gathering dusk.

THIRTY-SEVEN

◆

It was just nine-thirty on the following (Saturday) morning when John Masters and his wife slid their car smoothly into a parking place on the tree-lined main street of the little town of Ridgeham and got out to begin looking around. The village had never been large and it did not seem to be experiencing any great growth now. John guessed, except for the supermarket in the next block and the combination mini-mart and self-service gas station they had driven past coming into town, what he was seeing was very much the town his father had seen and known and grown up in. The houses were neat and well cared for, but few of them had been constructed since World War II.

John turned to his wife. "Where do we begin?

Jan laughed. "Why not try that old standby, 'the oldest living inhabitant.'"

John's eyes sought out the post office building across the street. "That's the place to start," he indicated.

"Not on Saturdays," she laughed.

"Then where?"

"If we were in New England, literary wisdom would lead me to the old cracker barrel in the Village Store. Next best thing might be the manager of the Supermarket?"

"Good enough," John agreed and they crossed the street and walked in through the double doors into aisles crowded with displays. It was obvious this was not the hour most of the residents chose to lay in supplies. One or two customers lounged in corners of the store, picking up items and depositing them in shopping carts pushed listlessly before them. Most of the activity was being carried on by young men and women in green aprons who were stocking, arranging, pricing, and otherwise looking busy, preparing the store for customers who would be arriving later in the day.

Near the check-out island stood a man in his early sixties talking earnestly to a couple of younger men. John and Jan drew near and stood waiting to be noticed by what they judged to be either the manager or owner. Seeing them, he dismissed his companions to their assigned tasks and turned to ask what was needed.

"Information. My father was born and raised here shortly after the turn of the century and I am looking for someone who might remember him and be able to give me information about him and the family."

"You're from a family around here? What was the name?"

"Masters. My grandfather was Allen Masters."

"Oh sure. Had the Feed and Seed Store down by the tracks. Used to buy pellets from him for my rabbits when I was a kid. Well, let's see. I would guess the best person for you to talk to would be old Mister Ewan."

Deep in the recesses of memory a chord sounded. "That wouldn't be 'Gary Ewan' would it?" John asked.

"Yeah, that's his name, though I don't think anyone alive calls him by his first name. Somethin' about him, we all just call him 'Mister Ewan'. He's in his eighties but he's spry and his mind is clear as a bell. I would think he could tell you whatever you might want to know."

"How would I find him?"

"He's sure to be at home, puttering around that old place of his, leastwise on a Saturday morning at this hour. Go on down this street here to the corner then turn right and it will be the last house at the end of the block." Gestures illustrated the words. "You been here before?"

"No, never have. Grew up out west, this is my first visit."

"Well, you might want to know, when you've turned the corner, the building across the street was your grandfather's store. The Kriegers own and run it now, of course, but it has hardly changed at all since I used to go in there more than fifty years ago."

They thanked him and made their way to the street, directing their steps according to his instructions. As they walked John shared his memories with her: "I remember dad talking about Gary Ewan. He was the kid who went with him to join the Navy. They were together that night and they signed up the next day in Rochester and went through 'boot camp' together. Then Gary was assigned to Naval Air when dad went to sea. Gary was killed in an accident a couple of years later."

"And so he is alive here. How do you suppose that happened?"

"I'm sure if we can get him to talking about dad he will tell us how things were different from what I remember being told, and we will be able to reconstruct what did or didn't happen that was different."

They had arrived at the neat old Victorian two-story house, freshly painted white with green trim, standing well back in a lovely well-tended garden. An elderly man was moving down the pathway maneuvering a wheelbarrow filled with a mixture of soil and fertilizer. When he saw the couple turning in at his gate he set the barrow down and came forward to greet them, brushing his hands off on his work pants.

"I sure hope I can help you folks, 'cause I'd like an excuse to talk instead of workin' this morning," he grinned. The name's Ewan." He thrust his hand at John.

"Glad to meet you, Mister Ewan. I'm John Masters and this is my wife, Jan."

He turned his handshake from John and presented his old brown hand to the beautiful woman standing beside him. "Well, this is a real pleasure," he said with just a hint of emphasis. "Yes indeed. Masters, eh? Any relation to the Masters family that lived around here?"

"Yes. Allen R. and June Masters were my grandparents."

"That so? Funny, I would've thought I knew all the young ones of that clan. You a boy of Howard's he has kept hidden all these years?"

"No. Howard is my uncle, I guess, though I never met him and haven't heard from him for years." In truth his father had never heard from either his brother or his sister, and he had rarely mentioned them. John had always believed by the time his dad had gotten back to the stream of family life after going into the Navy, the lives of his siblings had diverged from his own and gone their own way, so no one was too concerned about re-establishing the lines of communication. They all had other things more pressing to do than to write to relatives, however close, who no longer shared in life on any day-to-day basis.

The old man was looking at him, clearly waiting for some additional word. "I am Lewis Masters' son."

"No. Lewis' son? He's alive then?"

"Not now. He was. Went west and married when he got out of the Navy." John was skating on thin ice and knew it.

"He joined the Navy? After all, he went and did it." He shook his head. "Well, I guess that's the end of a lifetime of wonderin'."

"That's what I came to ask you about. Dad talked about his friend, Gary Ewan, who went with him when he ran away to join the Navy back then. But I'm not clear just what happened, and we've come three thousand miles to see if I can get it straight in my own mind."

"I'll tell you what I can, but I've never understood what took place that night, and I don't mind tellin' you what you've told me hasn't made it any easier."

"Would you please just tell me what happened as far as you were concerned. That would really be a great help."

The man motioned them to the old wooden lawn furniture on the broad front porch of the house. They seated themselves and the patriarch ran his hand over his rough face thoughtfully, then began.

"Lew and I were best friends. His house was just back to side with this one, 'round the corner there, and he worked with his dad across the street. Well, a few months after we graduated from high school things weren't goin' so good for either one of us. I had no job here in town, as the hardware store had just gone out of business and no hired work was available in the dead of winter, and Lew was just not hittin' it off with old Allen, his dad. So we got to talkin' about the Navy. The more we talked, the better it sounded to Lew, and whatever he decided I figured I'd go along with. Well, things went this way, with lots of talkin' and dreamin', until the seventeenth of February. Then Lew and Allen had a big row about somethin' over at the store. So next mornin' we made our plans. We decided to leave home that day and go to Rochester and enlist in the Navy. I was to walk over to Lymanville in the afternoon and arrange for the use of a room to sleep in that night at my cousin's house there. Meanwhile, Lew would wait until Frank Connelly got back from his run takin' the milk in to the plant at Overton. He'd be back around seven and he'd promised to have some money for Lew, about thirty dollars he'd borrowed from him. That was a lot of cash in those days and Lew wasn't goin' to leave without gettin' what was owed him. Well, anyway, after he got the money Lew was going to walk along the tracks to Lymanville and join me at my cousin's place, and then we thought to catch a ride into Rochester the next morning. It seemed a likely plan and I followed through on it."

"What happened?"

"Nothin'. He never showed up. I waited there all night, finally fell asleep in the chair and woke up at two-thirty in the morning with him still not there. I went to bed and slept in. Waited around until mid-morning and then walked down the tracks to see if I would meet him. Went on into town, comin' in right by the feed store. Old Allen was fumin' around, pretty unhappy about somethin' and when I asked for Lew he told me he had up and left. I looked all over town for him, but he wasn't there. That night Frank Connelly told me he had sure enough picked up the money and started toward the tracks leading out of town with a pack over his shoulder. Well, then I cadged a ride into Rochester and went to the recruiting station there and asked for him, but nobody by that name had ever been there. I waited to see if he would turn up and explain what happened, but he never did. And I have been waiting all these years, up until right now."

"Lewis left Frank Connelly at what time?"

"Oh, maybe about seven-thirty, as I remember him tellin'—maybe a mite later."

"Was it easy walking along the tracks?"

"There was a path ran along there. At night it wasn't fast walkin' but it wouldn't have been hard."

"But coming back the next morning along that right of way, didn't you encounter the famous explosion place?"

"Sure I did. There'd been a frightful bang the night before, though my cousin's place was in a kind of hollow and we didn't lose any windows. Folks around Lymanville thought maybe a locomotive had exploded. Yeah, there was a crowd and a lot of stuff and confusion I had to get through, but I was too concerned with what had happened to Lew to give any attention to what that was all about. When I was sure he wasn't in the crowd, I pushed on and kept walkin'."

In his mind's eye John could visualize that night. He could picture the young man who would have been his father walking through the star-studded darkness toward Lymanville, his arranged accommodations, and his waiting friend. Then suddenly and without warning the explosion had engulfed him, and ended his life. But the question was, how could this whole situation possibly be explained to the old friend sitting before him, who had spent a lifetime wondering about the inexplicable disappearance of what he thought to be his best friend?

As if to echo his thoughts the old man looked him directly in the eyes and demanded, "Well, what did happen?"

John shifted uneasily. "That's really what I came to discover. The only explanation I can offer is that dad was caught in that explosion and lost touch with himself for a while. He wandered off in a daze, I guess, and when he came to himself it was too late to go back and make contact. That's my best guess."

"And he never let me know what had become of him? I never did join the Navy. Allen hired me to fill in at the store until Lew might show up, and I worked there for six or seven months before I got a job in a lumberyard over between here and Medina. I've spent my life wondering about that night and figuring what could have happened to my best friend. I did think once maybe he had been caught in that explosion, 'cept they never found any sign of anybody bein' there. Now I find he just never bothered to let me know. Son, no offense, but I almost wish you hadn't come."

John felt the same way. "I'm sorry. I'm really sorry." There was nothing else to say. He couldn't say, ". . .but because of this you have lived another sixty years." Nor could he possibly relieve the old man's mind by telling him the truth of his friend's disappearance. Silently he and Jan arose and walked away. The old man did not even seem to notice their departure. He was staring at the Feed and Seed Building and the railroad track beyond.

THIRTY-EIGHT

◆

The path beside the railroad track was well worn and easy to walk. The midday sun was warm without being hot, and they walked in personal silence broken only by the random counterpoint of bird songs and distant truck and tractor noises. The railroad right-of-way had been here a long time and they walked past the fenced corners of field and meadow and through verdant copses and along the edges of orchards in sweet bloom.

With every step, John retraced the footsteps of his father on that fateful night. His father had told him of his nighttime departure from home but had not dwelt on the details of this walk. But the world where he heard his dad recount the events of that night and succeeding days was not the world where an explosion had ever shattered the calm of this bucolic place, nor where there had ever been such a things as an Invisible Radiating Anomaly. John was convinced now this was in fact the *Event* he had been seeking. That one cataclysmic moment was the difference between the world he had known and the world where he now found himself a stranger and virtual outcast. He glanced at his watch. He had started the stopwatch function as they left the town beside the feed store and started along the pathway beside the tracks. He did some quick calculations. If his dad had passed the point where he had started his watch at seven-forty, they had four more minutes to walk before they would come to the place where he would have been walking at eight-thirteen P.M., the moment when the great explosion had lit up the area and made its presence so fatally known. He deliberately did not look about or ahead to see where he might be or to what he was coming.

The time elapsed. He stopped and looked around.

Time had healed but not yet erased the evidence of what had happened here that night. The dead trees had long since been cleared away, and there was no sign the tracks had ever been disturbed; but there was still a great oval gap in the trees that surrounded the place, and the fused crust of earth still sealed the central part of much of the space where he was standing. John reached down and picked up a fragment of that crust. It was a very thin layer of a rough green glass overlaying and cementing together grains of the soil from which it had been so abruptly formed. He knew from his reading that the first arrivals at the site had found rails and ties and trees and all things had been replaced in the center of the blast area by this simple crust of irregular lustre.

He was standing at what must have been the virtual center of the explosion. He was sure he was standing close to the very spot where his father, the gruff, good-hearted but unpredictable source of generosity and discipline of his childhood, had been annihilated. At this place his mother's whole future had been changed, so she had married later and died early without ever bearing himself or any other child. At this place the lives of countless people had been changed in literally thousands and even tens of thousands of ways, great and small. Only he knew or could be aware of what changes had been wrought here. Only he had any knowledge of how the world had been without this event on that night so long ago.

He was sure now he was in fact alone. No one else had been close enough to the blast to be obliterated as his father had been. He felt sure there was in fact no other person besides himself wandering about homeless in the midst of familiarity. No other human body had contributed to the recipe for this vitreous crust.

But what was he seeing? He felt confident the I.R.A. had found its source here on that February night. But precisely what was it that had happened? Had some node, vortex or black hole been generated here, that in its birth had created such havoc and then drifted slowly westward, higher and higher, until at length it had either faded, been dissolved or drifted into the deadness of space, entirely away from its planet of origin? He thought of the battalions of scientists who had visited this spot over the years. The signs of their probing were in evidence all around him. This was now taken as the place where there had been a most strange meteorite impact; but it was clear to him the explosion was above the surface of the ground and not under it. Nor

179

could he forget the best witnesses had, in fact, stated flatly nothing preceded the explosion. There had been neither streak of light nor any sound that drew the eyes of those happening to be outside and looking to the place where the brightness and the shattering sound that followed would originate.

John had not been given to visiting his father's grave after his death. He had grieved for him but he had not felt any point in coming back to the place where the container his father had now discarded was slowly and invisibly returning to the earth from which it had been fashioned. But now John knew that grave and its marker did not exist, and this place and the glaze upon it was in fact the last resting place of his father's body. No one in the world but himself was aware that this marked the resting place of a life cut off and vaporized on the threshold of promise.

Once again he faced the question of his father's relationship to God and his ultimate fate. When the news had come of his aging father's sudden mortal heart seizure, he had faced the question with some feelings of guilt and regret, as if he might have exerted more influence over his strong-minded parent to bring him to some kind of spiritual transformation and visible conversion. He had then finally resolved to leave his father to the love of the God Who had created him and loved him more than any son could. He was then regretfully reconciled to leaving his father to the mercy of Christ at the judgment.

Now this was even more necessary. He reached out and grasped Jan's hands and stood facing her. She looked into his eyes and understood what she saw there and nodded.

"Let's pray," John began self-consciously. "O God, our Father, we lift up to you at this, the last place of living and the place of his dying, the soul and spirit of Lewis Allen Masters. Father, we do not understand what it was that happened here or how it has come to be; but we lift up the life here cut off in its prime, and ask for your mercy and love upon Lewis. We lift him up to You as the man whom we knew but now never was, an honest and loving father who did all he understood was required of him and lived in integrity and open commitment to his family all the days of his life. Into Your hands we commit his spirit and his soul in our trust that your mercy for him in the judgment shall reflect the fullness of Your knowledge and love. In Jesus' Name. Amen."

Silence. Nothing stirred, far or near. It was as if all things everywhere had stopped. Then Jan began to speak, strongly and with unusual urgency: "Have I not said, 'I will not leave you orphans?' You are my children and I have kept You in My hand. Because of your faithfulness all will be restored to you, and more than you have hitherto enjoyed, because you are trusting in Me. All that you can understand will be shown to you. You are My children. I am your Father. Go in peace."

Silence. John looked up into the tearful face of his prophet-wife. He drew her close to him and began kissing the tears away. She drew her body tight against his and lifted her face for a long and love-filled kiss, lip to lip and breath to breath.

And John thought of death no more. All of his thoughts and feelings were filled with life.

THIRTY-NINE

◆

The next two weeks proved to be a romantic interlude as they sped quickly by for John and Jan.

They drove into New England on what can only be described as their honeymoon. After an extended telephone conference with Denver and John's three friends, it was agreed John had learned as much as he could at the moment and they should reunite after Mothers' Day to discuss what had been achieved. Then they would decide where John might go and what he might do to try to restructure his life. Meanwhile, all agreed, a leisurely tour of New England would be helpful in laying a foundation for his new marriage to his well-remembered wife. There was no argument. John was clearly delighted just to be with Jan again; especially with this fresh, newly loving and responsive Jan, unspoiled by his former blundering in learning skills as a husband. For Jan, who would gladly have gone anywhere and done anything with her dream-husband, it was an added blessing that she had always wanted to see New England where so much of the history she had read had been made. So they left cares behind and lived for each other and the sights and experiences of the moment. In later years she would often laughing chide her husband that they should go back to New England to see what they had neglected to see, through being so absorbed in each other. They spent these days in journeying from point to point, in obedience to their role as tourists. Finally they drove to New York and caught an afternoon flight to Denver, arriving in the early evening.

Wes and Ruth Hammetson met them at the airport, taking them to the apartment that had been secured for them. John carried Jan across the threshold of what they identified as their first "home," to find Jim Braddock and Ken Baker already there, with food prepared and purchased for the belated wedding banquet and welcoming party. After the meal, the three women—Jan, Ruth, and Martha Braddock—retired to the kitchen to make motions toward the dishes but mostly to talk, get acquainted, and make the newcomer feel welcome. John told the three men everything he had discovered since he had left them at the airport on Holy Saturday four weeks earlier.

They were fascinated by the details of differences and the experiences through which John had passed. They listened carefully as he told of the beginnings of the identification of the I.R.A. as the *Event* that had in fact completely alienated his life from the lives of everyone around him. They each acknowledged they were aware of and had known about this strange object that had been isolated in the sky in its pathway across the country, though never really identified (except to be given the three word description from which the familiar acronym had been abstracted.) A decade ago they had wondered, as had the rest of the country's science buffs, about the nature of this then-publicized object; but as it became commonplace and attempts to determine its nature failed, questions about it and even its existence faded into the background of newer and more pressing considerations.

They looked with John at his well-used airline map with the pathway of the object traced between its known locations in the previous decade, its earlier pass over Henley and the various communities earlier in the century when outbreaks of "Camerapox" had been chronicled, ending with the explosion on February 18, at 8:13 P.M. sixty-five years ago— or rather, beginning there.

They wondered if John was, in fact, the first person who had ever associated that "meteor explosion," about which they had sometimes read in Sunday Supplement articles, with the origin of the Invisible Radiating Anomaly. None of them were accredited as scientists (although Jim Braddock's undergraduate degree had been in chemistry before he decided on ministry) but they could see that knowing this phenomenon had originated in a violent and fatal explosion did not do anything to explain what the thing actually was. Nor did it explain the strange lifetime experience of John Masters, who had seemingly been born and lived for forty-five years (less a few days) in a world where that explosion had never happened and the I.R.A. was never present in the sky.

Had not the women taken pity on a tired Jan and insisted their husbands leave the travelers to their rest, the discussion might have gone on until the early hours of Sunday morning. As it was, the door closed behind the departing friends a score of minutes after midnight and the exhausted couple retired with laughter and contentment to their first night in a place they expected would remain theirs for the foreseeable future.

The next morning was Mothers' Day and John and Jan were scheduled to attend services with Wes and Ruth at Jim Braddock's church, the familiar St. Matthew's, in whose sanctuary John had first come to himself. As they received a bulletin at the door, John noticed they were observing the practice of placing a rose on the altar in memory of each deceased mother of a member of the congregation. As might have been expected, the altar was thus a mass of roses, while nearby stood a tastefully lettered roster of the women thus memorialized. John shook his head over the problem this presented to him. He should have ordered a rose "in memory of Alice Wexler Liebman, mother of John L. Masters, killed in a motorcycle accident four years before he was born."

The service was well handled. It was sentimental without being maudlin; and in the midst of respect for motherhood, the sovereignty of God and the opportunity of Jesus Christ were lifted up. The music by the small choir was superb.

In the coffee hour afterward, Charlotte Black, Jim Braddock's secretary, approached the place where he, Jan, Jim and Martha Braddock, and Wes and Ruth all stood talking quietly together. "Doctor Braddock, that man called again about Reverend Masters a few minutes before the service was to begin."

John picked up on the mention of his name. "Someone called about me?"

Jim turned quickly. "Yes, John. Some fellow has been calling for two weeks or more. Wants to know when you'll be back and where he can find you. He won't give his name or what he wants. He just calls and when he finds you are still not here he hangs up without explanation. I don't like the sound of it."

John was puzzled. In a world where he had no official existence, who would be concerned about him and wanting to know his whereabouts and to be in touch with him?

"When did all this start?" he asked.

Charlotte glanced at her notebook. "On the morning of April 27th," she confirmed.

"That would have been the day we were in Albion, in New York," Jan noted.

"Have you any idea where he is calling from?"

"Not really, although I have the feeling the calls are long distance and not local," Charlotte answered. "But they are direct calls, not 'person-to-person'."

"And just exactly what does he say?" John's face showed his concern.

"He always begins, 'Is Reverend John L. Masters there?' Then, when I say 'no' sometimes he will ask when you are expected. Other times he just hangs up."

"Have you tried to find out what he wants of me?"

"Several times, but when I ask a question the line goes dead."

"Always the same voice?"

"As far as I can tell."

"And have you told him I would be here this next week?"

"No. At Doctor Braddock's instruction I have told him nothing about where you were or when you might be expected."

""ohn, in the circumstances I just don't know what this fellow might be about, so I felt the safest thing was to tell him nothing at all," Jim explained.

"And what did you tell him this morning?"

"I didn't know whether you were here yet or not."

At this point a parishioner came up to talk with her pastor, to congratulate him on the sermon just concluded, so the conversation ended. But John could not put the question of the mysterious caller out of his mind. Who in the world knew enough about him to want to call and get in touch with him? Was he, perhaps, the subject of some investigation? And if so, by whom?

FORTY

◆

The Masters' sojourn in their new home turned out to be short-lived.

That Sunday afternoon, at a "council of war" following a festive dinner, it was decided John and Jan and Ken Baker would fly the next morning to California to visit Berkeley, Hilltop Theological Seminary, and the University to attempt to get some help in understanding what they knew. Ken had attended the University as an undergraduate and he felt he could possibly be of help to John in making contact with a leading research physicist with whom the whole business of the I.R.A. and the explosion might be discussed. Also, in the light of John's blighted status at the seminary, it might be helpful for Ken to be along to run interference for him. Besides all this, Ken was ready for a few days away from his pulpit, and this was a fascinating opportunity for him.

So Monday, the 14th of May, found them winging over the arid brightness of the Utah desert enroute once again to California. As they flew, Jan took the opportunity to ask Ken about his unmarried status. She had learned from her husband about the wife to whom he had introduced Ken in that other life, and because of her own experience and happiness, she found herself intrigued by the situation. Ken understood her interest and motivation and talked easily about himself.

"It isn't that I haven't met some fine women or that I don't want to get married; it just has never worked out for me. Something always seems to happen to spoil things. No matter how interested I am or she may become, a circumstance arises, and it doesn't come to anything in the end."

"No dreams?" asked Jan, remembering her own vivid dream life.

186

"No, not particularly. None at least like yours." They had all been interested in Jan's account of her life and her shock and joy at finding the literal "man of her dreams" standing on her doorstep late that night before her wedding.

"I must admit when John first mentioned the name 'Valerie DuMennier' I felt a twinge of almost familiarity with it, as if somehow it was the name of a person once important but for a long time unremembered and forgotten. For that brief moment it was quite an experience. But I can't remember dreaming about any particular girl with that name, and for the life of me I cannot recall where I could have heard it before."

"But every time you begin to get serious about some woman, circumstances spoil it and you are left a bachelor?"

"That's the way it works. And I'm not lucky at cards either," he added ruefully.

Jan smiled. "But I have to wonder about Valerie. What is her situation?"

"If John is right about the woman he remembers her to be, then we would expect her to have been married long since." He looked at the mature loveliness sitting beside him and flushed. "I mean, well—beautiful women who want to be married don't usually remain unmarried..."

Jan laughed disarmingly. "And my dreams and their results were pretty unusual. I know what you mean, Ken. But I have been thinking about all of this. I believe my husband. I think all he remembers is true and his life was real. So when what he calls "the Event" —I suppose this I.R.A. thing—happened, everything was changed except his memories and existence. But he and I were married. In the eyes of God we had become 'one being together.' No matter what changed, we still were one in God's sight and so He undertook to keep me for John and I was very successfully deterred from marrying anyone else and committing some kind of unwitting cosmic adultery, by means of my dreams. I can't tell you what those dreams meant to me or what they did to my waking emotional life. I would get up from a night when I had dreamt of John to walk through the day comforted and blessed by remembering what I had felt from his presence. And, most of the time, there was nothing erotic or even sensual about those dreams. It was his presence as a person and the feeling I had about him rather than what he did in those dreams, usually, that made the difference. I have to believe my dream life was the way God preserved me against that day when I would be found by him and have my true marriage restored."

"I can't argue with that."

"But John says you have been married—or were married—almost as long as we were. So, if this is true for John and me, then it might—must—also be true for yourself and Valerie. If I am right, we will find Valerie unmarried and awaiting you, or at least unusually open to meeting and getting acquainted and becoming married."

Ken laughed and shook his head. "I like your theory even if I find it difficult to get up any great faith in its fulfillment."

"Would you mind, really, if I try to give it a chance? May I attempt to find her and bring her to you?"

Ken looked at the sparkling joy in her face and wondered what she could ask that he would deny. "Jan, you are free to do anything you can. It is just, at my age, I have stopped having any great hope any woman will be found to share my life."

John, who had been listening with interest in spite of the news magazine he was holding, leaned across his wife from the aisle side. "Never underestimate....rother. I think it will be an interesting experiment to see what Jan can accomplish."

They flew in silence then for some time. Finally Jan excused herself and made her way forward in the aircraft. Ken watched her go and then leaned again over to John across the now empty seat. "Do you agree with this 'marriages are made in heaven' outlook your wife seems to hold?"

John laughed. "I don't think it is quite that. Jan isn't saying marriages are some kind of predestined pairing conceived in the beginning and forced upon us by some eternal decree. But when marriages do happen, they involve a divine reality that must then be noted and honored in heaven. She's pretty obviously been doing some deep thinking about her—our—situation, and she feels what is true of us will also be true of you. And maybe it's more than just her thinking: remember, she has received and is exercising the gift of prophecy."

Ken's face mirrored his wariness. "That's another thing you two seem set upon that I just am not sure of. Do you mean by that she has received some special skill in predicting the future?"

John shook his head vigorously. "No, not at all. A prophet may, of course, have to talk about what will be in order to convey the message given; but basically prophecy is telling the will and purpose and direction of God to selected people in a given situation so they may know and heed and obey. It really is not involved with 'future-telling' and is as remote as anything can be from those 'psychics' who publish in the tabloids and call their utterances 'prophecy'."

"Do you think there is any chance of our finding this Valerie and of my marrying her?"

"On the basis of what has been happening to me I think there is an excellent chance you will find her, and then the rest will be up to what you and she freely decide after you meet each other. I think I agree with Jan; the fact that you two were married before the Event for two decades will be more important than can be accounted for on the basis of ordinary human cause-and-effect experience."

"O.K. Then let me ask you, is Jan the same woman now you remember being married to?"

John, smiling, paused. "No, and yes," he said slowly. "She is the same basic person she always was, but there is a new strength and depth, a loving vitality that I did not notice in her before. Part of it is that I am a better husband now than I started out being when we were married 'before', but there is more difference than just that. She is just somehow more aware and purposeful than I ever remember her being on any sustained basis."

Ken shook his head wonderingly. "Well, if we do find this Valerie and the magic happens for us and I finally find a wife to share my life the way Jan shares yours, then you will make a real believer out of me."

John had been watching and slid out of his seat to facilitate his wife's return. As he reseated himself he leaned over and quickly kissed her. Jan looked quickly from one to the other and laughed and took a magazine out of the seat pocket, settling back to read in that self-conscious way an attractive woman has when she knows those around her are watching.

Ken settled back and spent some minutes hoping this prophet was right and some comparable person was somewhere ahead in space and time, awaiting their arrival.

Coming down at San Francisco International Airport is always an exercise in turmoil and it proved so again this day. The seemingly endless corridors, the wait with anxious anticipation for the eventual return of their luggage, and the rental and procurement of an automobile to use in their Bay Area stay took time, effort, and Christian grace to endure with fortitude. It was thus after noon when the trio drove through the light midday traffic over the Bay Bridge and into the East Bay. Ken noticed John was well versed in these freeways and he remembered far better than Ken himself which off-ramp to take to lead them into Berkeley and the area where Hilltop Theological Seminary was located. In the center of town they turned off into the driveway of a motel, and Ken and Jan waited in the car while John rented two adjoining rooms for their use.

After the whirlwind activity of unpacking and the freshening delight of a quick shower and clean clothes, they were ready for their return to the familiar walls of the seminary that had forgotten John completely.

FORTY-ONE

◆

Again, if the Reverend Ken Baker had ever had any doubts about John Masters and his knowledge of Hilltop Theological Seminary, they were thoroughly dissipated by the events of that afternoon. He walked silently beside John as John identified places and occurrences that were often thus recalled to him after twenty years of being forgotten. John pointed out the exact place where Ken's disabled car had for so long sat before it was finally hauled away on order of the town fathers. They walked down the hill and saw where the ice creamery had been whose products he had so regularly consumed during his stay on campus. They walked through the dormitory building while John recalled with accuracy the three-year history of each room when Ken was himself a student here.

There were, of course, discrepancies. The room John had occupied was remembered by Ken as being used by another. Out of this, perhaps, had grown another disparity: the eruption in the married students' apartments that Ken could remember vividly, but of which John knew nothing. It had taken place in his senior year, Ken recalled. One of the men had suddenly "broken down" and begun to behave irrationally and violently, and had to be forcefully subdued by the police summoned by seminary authorities. John could recall no such occasion. Had it then happened because of something John had not been present to prevent, or was it perhaps due to the presence in the community of someone who would not have been there had John been in residence? The question fascinated Ken even as it awed him. John was used to this kind of consideration by now and merely added it to the growing list of such questions he expected to spend the rest of his life pondering.

191

John was unerring in describing changes in buildings and other features that had been altered since their days as students here. His powers of observation and his memory made him better aware of such things than was Ken, so between the two of them if either were thought to have been merely an interloper and perhaps a frequent visitor rather than an alumnus, Ken would have been the one deemed best to fit that role. And yet, of course, the registrar's office knew nothing of any John Lewis Masters of the same class as Ken's, or of any other year. It was John who first recognized several faculty members of their own time at the seminary whom they encountered that afternoon, but it was Ken they in turn recognized and spoke to. After each encounter John would describe with greatest accuracy the personal impression and idiosyncrasies each manifested in the lecture room.

If the truth be told, before this afternoon Ken Baker had believed John because of the confidence shown by Jim Braddock and Wes Hammetson. He himself had formed an opinion that John was probably "all right" but his feelings were that this man could not logically be what he was putting himself forward as being, and so he was not totally convinced in his own heart. But now those doubts vanished completely. He came to feel and to understand the pain and perplexity of the other's situation; and to be newly driven to do whatever he could to find the answers to how this had come about. Failing that, at least he now resolved to do whatever he could personally to ease that pain. As he was just becoming aware of this new decision in himself, they rounded a bend in the hall of the Administration Building and came face to face with Doctor Edith Canning, long-time professor of Theology. Recognizing Ken, she greeted him warmly, inquiring about his church, life, and welfare with obvious real interest.

Ken interrupted the ritual pleasantries with an abrupt request, "Doctor Canning, have you a few moments to speak with us and discuss a problem?"

She glanced at her watch. "Is it important, Mr. Baker?" It was clear if this had been a student rather than an alumnus, she would have expected him to schedule an appointment at some later time.

"I think it is most vital and necessary that we talk to you, and I don't think I can overemphasize its importance." He stole a glance at John to find him tense and expectant.

The elderly theologian smiled and relaxed. "Well, my housekeeper may not understand the delay, but sometimes these things cannot be helped. Let's step back to my office." She led the way down the hall to a door she opened with a key from her purse. They entered, settling on invitation into comfortable chairs with which, in addition to a desk and many books, this faculty study was furnished.

"Now," she said directly, "what is this grave matter for which you need my counsel and advice?" Her whole attention was fixed upon Ken and she looked not at all at his companion.

"Doctor, why have you not greeted another of your students, the Reverend John Masters, who was a classmate of mine?" His tone was almost accusing.

She looked at Ken with surprise and then at John with intensity. "I am sorry to say I do not recognize your face, though I am aware it may have changed somewhat in nineteen years; but I also do not know your name. If you had been a student of mine, I do not think I would forget that. How should I know you, sir?"

John spoke quietly. "What Ken says is quite true. In my own memory and experience, I remember vividly, in my 'Middler' year here, sitting under you in Systematic Theology and learning a very great deal. I remember being amazed at the way you would answer even the most difficult questions asked of you in the classroom. Other professors, when unexpectedly asked a highly technical or difficult question, would hem and haw and obviously be thinking on their feet and have to formulate an answer. You always seemed to have the most complicated answers to the most terrifying questions already formulated and analyzed in your mind and on the tip of your tongue. I cannot tell you how much your teaching has affected my thinking and living and the content of my faith in the past twenty years."

"This is all very gratifying to hear, Mr.—Masters, is it?—but why is it I do not remember you? I take pride in my ability to remember each of my students."

John smiled. "That is the question to which Ken had reference. I am convinced that, had I come to see you two months ago, you would have had no trouble remembering me and calling me by name. Now there is no one anywhere who seems to have that ability. I have some information about what has happened to me but I cannot begin to understand how it happened. I know I spent three years here at Hilltop. I graduated and have served in a succession of churches in this United Connectional Annual Conference. But for the past month and a half everyone reacts as you are reacting to me; not recognizing me and knowing nothing of anything I have ever done or anywhere I have been."

She was looking directly at him now with level, piercing eyes. "I shall have to hear more about all this. Please start from the beginning."

And he did.

FORTY-TWO

♦

John started at those latest moments of the old life he could remember and then went on to his awakening in Denver and the discovery, bit by bit, of what had happened to him. He told of his travels and investigations and the things he had observed that differed from what he remembered. He told of becoming aware of the I.R.A. phenomenon he was sure had not been a part of the world when he had attended the seminary and her classes. He told of the visit to New York State and what he had found there. He told her of Jan and of her dreams. He told everything.

When John had completed his narration Doctor Canning turned her eyes to Ken. He replied to the question she did not have to voice.

"I am sure this is all true. John knows this campus at least as well as I do and, if anything, better. He remembers so much about me and my time here I have to believe him. I cannot begin to understand how it could be true, but Wes Hammetson is convinced and so am I."

"So Wes is in this, too? Well, I must say I am also convinced of the sincerity and the sanity of Mr. Masters, and therefore I have to take seriously what he has told me. But I think we need help with this Invisible Radiating Anomaly aspect. I have a friend at the University who has made that his specialty over the years and is perhaps the leading expert on the whole question. Let me call him this evening and try for an appointment sometime tomorrow, when we can discuss this whole matter with him."

"Then you agree I am not insane?" John asked quietly.

"Insanity involves one of three kinds of disturbance," came the immediate reply. "A physiological disturbance in the metabolism affecting the brain and causing abnormal feelings and hallucinations; a personal aberration in the soul, when the pain of past memories comes to interfere with present perceptions and the ability to cope with reality; or the interference of some entity within the realm of the spirit that makes difficult, or even perhaps impossible, the willing control of our lives according to our own values, goals, and standards. Clearly none of these factors are at work in your situation or attitude, and we must seek the solution in reality rather than in some therapeutic response to pathology. No, Mr. Masters—John—you may count me as one of your 'believers.'"

She took John's telephone number at the motel; then quickly ushered them out of the office, leaving them standing in the corridor while she hurried to catch up with her interrupted schedule.

"I know I am not insane," John said as they watched her retreating form, "but I can't help being afraid others will jump to that conclusion."

They did not linger after that, but returned to the motel and to Jan. They found her surrounded by the large telephone directories for the greater Bay Area. She confessed she had been completely unsuccessful in finding any listing for Valerie DuMennier. "I'm afraid I don't know quite what to do next to try to find her."

John laughed. "Jan, if you are right in what you were saying to Ken on the plane then we need to pray for and expect divine help. Remember, none of this that has happened or will happen is a surprise to God. He is at work in our lives for His loving will, guiding, nudging, directing through love and obedience and circumstance in a vast matrix of lives in both time and space. God knew from the beginning of the world where we would be tonight and what we would be doing. He knows where Valerie is and what her situation would be. And He has always been aware of this entire I.R.A. *Event* and its consequences. The one ingredient we have to contribute to Him is our prayer and obedience. I would suggest we pray."

"What do you think we should be praying for?" Ken asked.

"The fulfillment of God's purpose in you and in Valerie through His grace."

And so they did pray. Through the time of silence and John's simple spoken prayer, Ken waited to see what Jan might say or do, expecting that as a "prophet" she might demonstrate her gift. But she remained silent and the prayer ended in simple words of confidence and thanksgiving.

The only thing Jan said was to call their attention to the hour and to the need for dinner. Ken recommended a popular seafood restaurant, thriving since their seminary days. They quickly got ready and made their way there. As always, the place was crowded and it was apparent they would have to wait for a table. Rather than stand about in the swarming entryway, Ken and John went into a garden courtyard where a fountain splashed and there were chairs and benches for those awaiting accommodations. Jan, in the manner of women everywhere, left them to seek out the Ladies' Room, presumably for last minute and totally unnecessary adjustments to her face.

The whole establishment was crowded with a number of parties as well as many couples awaiting dinner. John and Ken stood talking about inconsequential things and waiting for Jan's return. Finally they saw her coming through the clusters of people, accompanied by another woman.

"Ken, here is a woman who is moving to the Denver area and needs some advice on where to look for a place to live."

Ken looked at them inquiringly.

Jan caught the look and laughed. "Well, she is with a party waiting inside. It's a farewell celebration in her honor since she has taken a new job in Denver, and I just happened to be going by as she was saying she wished she knew someone she could ask about her new home. She has had the experience of moving into a neighborhood and then finding it was not as desirable as it had appeared. I knew you were familiar with Denver and thought you perhaps could help her."

Jan turned to the woman who now stood beside her. "This is Reverend Ken Baker who has a church in the Denver suburbs."

The stranger was looking at Ken with great intensity, as he was looking at her. Both were silent, preoccupied.

Jan looked at them and then at John, whom she found to be grinning broadly. For a moment no one spoke.

John broke the silence. "Ken, Jan, I would like you both to meet Miss Valerie DuMennier, the woman I have told you so much about."

At the mention of her name the woman's eyes momentarily wavered from him, but immediately returned to Ken. Then, after a moment she roused herself and turned to John.

"How did you know my name? I don't know you."

John smiled. "Valerie, that is a very long story. It begins with the time you and Donna went to that Alvaro Marini recital together. Do you remember how much you enjoyed it? Well, I would be interested in knowing if there was any feeling of disappointment, of feeling somehow let down by that evening?"

Valerie faced John with all seriousness. "And I would be interested in knowing how you know about that—how you know about me?"

John's face was steady. "Because in my memories, shared now by no other living person, I went to that concert also with a friend of mine and we sat next to you. During and after the concert we became acquainted. My friend fell in love with you and you with him. I remember being the best man at your wedding. I remember visiting in your home. I remember literally hundreds of things that no one else now has experienced and that have not, in fact, taken place. You see, I suffer from Omnesia. Everybody has forgotten me completely. Valerie, I know how strange and impossible all of this sounds."

"Outrageous is the word that occurs to me. How did you learn these things about me and what do you hope to accomplish with this story?"

"Valerie, who in all the world but yourself and Donna—wherever she may be by now—would know that as an encore that night Mr. Marini sang a song you love and that he never had recorded and we didn't even suspect was in his repertoire. It was "When Night Descends in Silence" by Rachmaninoff. Do you recall how surprised and delighted you were over the performance he gave? No detective prying into someone's life could come up with this kind of information. I haven't violated your privacy and would not do so, believe me. It is just that I can remember being there. Now let me ask you a very personal and important question. Why are you still unmarried?"

Jan spoke quickly. "This next Thursday it will be a month since John appeared on my doorstep late at night and told me his story of remembering me and being married to me. It is a great mystery and even a great tragedy, but it is no trick. There is no plan or plot here."

Valerie turned to Jan and spoke forcefully: "And what did you do when he told you these things?"

Jan laughed. "I ended up marrying him– and I don't regret it. Please trust us if you cannot believe him."

"And please answer the question," John added quietly. "Why is a beautiful woman like you not married?"

Valerie looked down. "You were right. I can remember a real sense of disappointment that night after the concert, as if somehow something that should have happened had not taken place." She looked again at

Ken Baker. "I have just never met a man with whom I wanted to spend my life. I'm not interested in marriage, I guess. That's all I can tell you because that's all I have been able to tell myself or any of my friends."

"No dreams?" Jan asked.

"What do you mean?"

"Well, in my case, I used to dream of John so frequently and emotionally that no flesh-and-blood man could compete with my dream experiences."

"I would say I don't dream, but scientists seem assured that everybody does; so all I can say is, I do not remember dreaming. I just have never found anyone yet I truly wanted to spend my life with."

"Exactly my feeling," interjected Ken. "People you went out with once or twice, persons nice enough but really somehow not quite right, if you know what I mean."

"Yes, precisely."

A man came pushing through the crowd to them at this moment. "Valerie dear, they have our room ready and everyone else is going in. I am delegated to come and get the guest of honor."

John was about to say something about saying good night and expecting to see her in Denver, when he noticed the real pain in the eyes of both Ken and Valerie at the interruption. Valerie made a visible decision and turned to the newcomer.

"Ed, go back and make sure there are three more places set. I have some very important friends who are joining us."

As her friend turned in bewilderment to go back and execute this latest complication, Valerie turned back to them smiling. "I can't let you go, I just can't. I don't know how I could believe a story such as I have heard, but I am unable to disbelieve it either. What you have told me about that night is true, and I am sure no one knew how much I enjoyed the singing of that one song. It has come, over the years, to have a special and personal meaning to me with its sense of loss and loneliness. Please be my guests tonight, and after the party let's talk about all of this more. I want to know everything."

"Why not just add Ken to your party and let us fend for ourselves?" Jan asked.

Valerie flushed and unexpectedly her eyes filled with tears. "It will raise fewer questions if you all come. And I do want to talk to all of you later on, but. . ."

Ken spoke again, in a barely audible voice. "If it will help, Valerie—

199

Miss DuMennier—I'll tell you I may have finally discovered in only the last few minutes what they mean about 'falling in love.' I have found the 'confirmed old bachelor' isn't quite as confirmed as he thought."

She could only nod and smile and blink. Reaching out, she took his hand and drew Ken with her toward the dining room where her friends were waiting. John and Jan followed.

"Isn't this the most remarkable coincidence?" asked Jan, happily.

"Dearest, you will have to learn there is one word that does not exist for the Christian. There is no such thing as coincidence. We call it 'providence.'"

FORTY-THREE

♦

However important that dinner turned out to be for Valerie and Ken, the really important one as far as John was concerned took place almost exactly twenty-four hours later in the home of Professor Edith Canning.

At her invitation they were all there. When they had finally returned to the motel the night before, a message had been waiting for them from Doctor Canning, indicating the meeting she had promised with her physicist-expert friend would be preceded by dinner in her own house. It had by then become necessary the following morning to call and advise her there would be four of them; John and his wife, and Ken and the woman who seemed already to be virtually his fiancée. The day was spent with John and Jan exploring together those features of the area with which she had once been familiar but now had never seen. Ken was, of course, helping Valerie with her last-minute preparations for the now doubly-important move to Colorado. Indeed, there was doubt for a time whether the newly assembled twosome would remember the dinner at all; but in the nick of time they turned up, laughing and clearly reveling in each other's company.

So Edith Canning welcomed two couples of mature, joyful guests to her home and discovered that for them it had become another Cana, richly blessed by a miracle of God. There was no wine served at all (since all present but Valerie were members of a denomination that traditionally abstained from alcohol) but it would have seemed to an observer that Christ had turned the prosaic food of the meal into some potent elixir, for there was joy and laughter and a sense of exultation beyond any dinner party Edith Canning could remember.

With the dinner over and coffee in hand, they retired to the study in the professor's rambling house, and there were joined presently by a bespectacled and balding man whom Doctor Canning introduced as Doctor Vladmir Hilding. He was a slight man, well under average height, whose ruddy cheeks contrasted with quick dark eyes set under bushy dark eyebrows. "Mild mannered, but intense," John thought to himself.

Doctor Hilding was, it seemed, Professor of Theoretical Physics at the University and a recognized international authority in the study of the Invisible Radiating Anomaly. He had directed the attempts to discover the nature of the phenomenon and had coordinated the gathering and interpretation of data concerning it from the time of its discovery until its disappearance just forty-five days previously. When he had received his coffee and was comfortably seated, John, at Edith Canning's invitation, began to relate his strange story once again.

He began with what he now considered to be the unfinished sermon, interrupted by temporary oblivion on Sunday, April 1st, and concurrent with the disappearance of the I.R.A. from earthly detection systems. He told of his awakening in Denver and his abrupt discovery that he was himself an anomaly, a person whose very existence had been forgotten by everyone connected with him. He told of the differences he had observed in events that now were recorded, compared with his own memories. He told of his first discovery of the Invisible Radiating Anomaly in that twice-weekly paper in Henley, and the surprise that was his in becoming aware of the whole I.R.A. phenomenon. He remembered nothing of any such thing from his own past and was sure had any such disturbance been detected and the reports about it published, he would have noticed and remembered. He got out his map and showed the crude line he had drawn on it and how the end of that line seemed to go to Ridgeham, the village where his father had been born and raised.

John told then of the conversation by the lakeside that early morning when he became aware for the first time of the "meteor-fall" near Ridgeham sixty-five years before. He described his reading about that event in the old local newspaper accounts during the visit to western New York State. He told of the interview with Gary Ewan and how it contrasted with the account of that long-remembered night as told by his father. He even mentioned the agitation in the canine population in the hours and days immediately following the explosion as reported by the local newspapers. He consciously tried to relate every scrap of information he had managed to gather in the month and a half since he had suddenly dropped out of his old life into this new one.

Professor Hilding listened quietly, only his eyes moving alertly behind the thick lenses of his glasses. When John had at last finished, he drew out a pipe, filled and lit it, then leaned back and spoke thoughtfully in a slightly accented voice that betrayed his birth perhaps somewhere in

eastern Europe.

"Edith, I want to thank you for inviting me here this night to meet this extraordinary gentleman and to hear this account. I don't know whether I will be able to help him the way he has helped me, but I shall try. I came here tonight with several theories competing in my mind to become the explanation for this major area of my work and study for the past ten years. As a result of what I have just heard I shall have to discard all of them but one.

"Let me review with you, for your information and for the benefit of my thinking, the data we have.

"There was a mysterious object. We called it the 'Invisible Radiating Anomaly,' and for good reason. This thing was 'invisible' because, while we were able to pinpoint its location, we could see nothing by radar or by optical means where it was supposed to be. Telescopes would not focus upon an object, and radar screens remained blank. It wasn't that we could 'see through it' exactly; we just did not see anything.

"It was 'radiating', as you know, X-rays, along with Ultraviolet and some radio-frequency transmissions. But what you may not realize is that it did not behave as it should, even as a radiating body. Radiations should be diminishing in proportion to the square of the distance, but this was not the case with the I.R.A. As you are aware, it was rising in its trajectory; and when we first detected it, it was nearing the atmospheric limit of the earth. It was in that part of the stratosphere where meteors begin to heat and flare on their entry. But in the ten years we studied it, it did not decrease its radiation to our ground stations. It actually seemed slightly to increase in the strength of its radiations. Incidentally, I am not surprised that, close to the ground, it also radiated high-pitched sound intensely disturbing to dogs, though inaudible to people.

"Now it was, of course, an 'anomaly' because we would not explain it. It was a node, a natural discontinuity, a specifically locatable aberration. Until this very night I do not believe anyone could have said for sure what it was. But now, I think I can tell you about what its nature is and what has happened to so affect your life..." He stopped to refill and relight his pipe, while they waited impatiently.

Finally he resumed. "Let me tell you what I have concluded. The newspaper accounts to which you refer were finally right, after all. This was a kind of meteor, a piece of debris falling to earth from deepest space. That much is true. We will never know what its precise composition was, because we have no way of examining anything like it and we have only theoretical awareness that matter like this can exist. A piece of perhaps similar cosmic stuff fell in Siberia in 1908 in another mystery we have never solved to our complete satisfaction, although the public may think otherwise. You know, of course, all of the matter with which we are familiar in our galaxy is made up basically of protons and positrons at the nucleus, with electrons in the shells around that central nucleus.

"I am quite sure you have also heard speculations about so-called 'Contra-Terrene Matter,' known simply as 'CT,' in which the electrons would provide an essentially negative nucleus about which positive particles would be arranged. This would be the exact reversal of our kind of matter and could, in theory, be similarly structured into as many elements as we have in our own universe, except every particle that is positive here would there be negative, and every negative one would there be positive. There could be gases and solids and liquids and metals, just as we have, but structured in exactly the opposite way our elements are arranged. Do you follow? This has been discussed mathematically and has been speculated about in science and science-fiction circles for years.

"Two entirely different kinds of matter, but completely unable to co-exist with each other. If such CT substance came in contact with our own matter, in whatever amount or circumstance, each would annihilate the other in an enormous release of energy. At least, this has been the theory. No one had ever actually seen it happen. Or, perhaps we must now say, no one ever had until that night sixty-five years ago, and your father—the man who should have been your father—did not live to tell what he saw.

"For I believe that is exactly what happened that night. A piece of CT matter came into contact with sufficient normal matter mass, and mutual annihilation resulted in a catastrophic explosion. Simple?

"But not so simple, I think. For there was one further difference between this meteor and our own earth that makes the situation enormously more complex. You know, of course, we now believe all matter in the cosmos came into existence in one vast 'Big Bang' perhaps some fourteen billion years ago. All of the billions of galaxies came into existence—or at least the stuff for them and the energy that made all subsequent events possible—at a point where time began and all things came into sudden being, with the potential of becoming what we now see all about us. Edith and I have spent many a long hour discussing this event and its significance for her and her students. But this Big Bang established something else beside the nature of our matter and the energy potential from which everything else has come. It established, also, what we must call 'the vector of time.' Here we have to rely upon the constructs of mathematical physics. We talk about a 'vector' because in our calculations we have discovered time is not simply the 'then-to-now' progression that we experience, like drops of rain running down a window pane. Our equations make it seem as if time may also have a 'direction' and a 'velocity,' a speed, that is established in the moment the Big Bang erupts and brings our space-time reality into existence. We cannot ourselves be aware of this for we have no way of measuring the direction of this thing that we call 'time.' We are carried along in it, and all other things with which we are connected are likewise taken along with us, like leaves and twigs being swept in a current of water. Since we cannot see 'the banks' or anything stationary by which to measure our rate and establish our direction of movement, we are unaware there is any movement or direction at all, or that there is any possibility of moving at a different speed and in a different direction.

"We have, of course, Einstein's General Field Theory and its subsequent amplification and modifications; but this theory is concerned only with what holds true in our reality, the result of our own Big Bang. But we have already had occasion to give it some further thought: Suppose that somewhere—or should I say 'somewhen?'—there is another Big Bang, another reality separate from our own that erupts into existence. Suppose there are formed in it also all of the materials for swarms of galaxies, with stars and worlds; and all of the energy that will bring them into organization and being and sustained functioning existence. Suppose that it bursts forth from wherever it comes from in a moment of beginning similar to the one we postulate for ourselves.

"Perhaps it would help if we can picture one of those glorious bursting fireworks that we see in public displays on the Fourth of July. A rocket streaks high in the sky and then bursts, throwing out thousands of brightly burning pieces in all directions from the center of the explosion. This is our Big Bang, our reality. Now picture a second such rocket bursting nearby so some part of its display comes into the expanding sphere of the first explosion.

"But now suppose this other cosmos is made of CT matter—no great wonder, this is the way in its first moment that matter begins to organize itself there, and in theory one form of matter is as likely as the other—and let us suppose also that the time vector that is established there is contrary to our own. This is virtually impossible for us to imagine. There is no other way to say it and we cannot conceive of it really in any kind of visual terms.

"Now let us understand that a small piece of matter, of debris out of that other cosmic event, in some way wanders or is somehow thrust into the midst of our own reality and is finally drawn to the earth and begins to fall as any other meteor would fall. Now as this object descends, it is itself moving in a time vector that is alien to ours and at least 'largely opposite' to that time flow we unknowingly experience. This object—a very small object, really—seems to us to be coming both out of space and time, out of our own future. It enters the atmosphere of the earth on Sunday morning just a few moments before noon, Pacific Standard Time, on April 1 of this year. As it begins to come in contact with that very attenuated matter on the edge of space, a plasma envelope generated by the breakdown of the surface atoms immediately forms in the rarified upper atmosphere, and this isolates the two kinds of matter from each other and delays the potentially great energy release that will take place where that piece of CT matter fully encounters our own. In terms of its own time vector, the object falls with normal acceleration, striking in a wooded area near a little town in New York State, where it finally is completely and explosively annihilated. Its time of transit from entry to impact is perhaps three hundred sixty seconds—six minutes, with the plasma envelope generated in the upper atmosphere protecting the bulk of the object from annihilation until it actually strikes the ground. What remains of the thing—as I said, a really very small piece perhaps the size of a marble—explodes with the violence of a small atomic bomb.

"But from our viewpoint this object enters from our future and impacts in our past. It comes into our awareness early in its flight and we are then able to observe its entry with the necessary impression it is making its exit. The nature of the radiation is explained by the Doppler effect that its time direction has upon the radiations from the plasma shield and the light that it is actually radiating, but it is in truth a Doppler effect in the time vector that we have, of course, never seen before and cannot imagine as existing. So the very nature of our past is changed by an intruder from the future. From your account, I cannot doubt the young man who would indeed have been your father was caught up and totally destroyed in the violence of that explosion. From that point on, all things rearranged themselves naturally, and events proceeded without your father and his participation—and of course, your own."

"Just where and when do we look for this 'other cosmos'—this other Big Bang?" asked John. "If its 'time vector' is the opposite of our own, it must come from our own future. Is this not so?"

"Those questions 'when' and 'where' are meaningless in this situation. If it was an event in our own reality that launched it on its fateful course, then it would of course share in our own time vector and we would simply see a meteor fall, with the object falling visibly to earth after traversing the heavens. But this is not a part of our reality at all. It is strictly not a part of 'our future' at all. It is best talked about using such words as 'otherwhen' and 'otherwhere.' The remarkable thing is that even a small piece escaped from that reality into this one," the professor replied.

"But why did it move so slowly across our skies?" John asked.

"That is the most baffling and intriguing part. I said before, such a meteor might require as much as six minutes to accomplish such a fall through our atmosphere, a trajectory of some three thousand miles. But the time vector of the object is contrary to the time vector of our own reality, and clearly its magnitude is also vastly greater. In those perhaps 360 seconds of its fall, the object moved three thousand miles and more through space and something like two billion seconds back in earth time. You can see the vast difference in those time vectors."

"Is such a difference possible? It would seem about five and a half million to one, when compared with our own time." said John.

"What is indeed possible or even usual we cannot know. This is the first and perhaps the last time that we have observed the results of any time vector other than our own. And our experience of our own time is entirely subjective and unrelated to the 'time vector' as it exists for our reality. How many other realities have come to exist, and what is the 'normal magnitude and direction' of their time vectors? We cannot know, nor may we even guess. All we have is the data from this one probably infinitely rare event, this random straying piece of another reality."

"But Vladmir," Edith Canning broke in, "how would such a body—a CT Meteor from another reality—break into our Creation? We are not talking about phenomena that are occupying neighboring space, on whatever scale at all, according to your science. Your image of the adjacent sky-rockets is vivid but certainly too simple for the real situation. Where did this thing 'come from' and how did it enter? Could it have found its way in through one of your cosmologist's 'Black Holes'?"

The professor turned to his old friend and paused pensively. "A good question, Madame Theologian. No, I do not think it made entrance through a Black Hole, for the behavior that we have measured indicates it is surely subject to the influence of gravity and a Black Hole is the ultimate gravity-trap from which nothing can escape. Nor do I believe it could have come through a 'White Hole' such as some of my colleagues are postulating. I believe this is a unique event and that ultimately we may yet witness a major cosmic dislocation that will take place at its arrival."

"Because, of course, that event lies in our cosmic future," John said, "and we must await its happening."

"Of course," agreed the Professor, "but we will certainly find ourselves waiting far longer than is practical. Remember the value that we estimate for the discrepancy in the time-vectors. The awaited event may well take place long after the earth and the solar system and even the galaxies have slowed and cooled and lapsed into that final 'cold-death' that is the ultimate fate of our cosmos. I am sure it will be most spectacular, but almost certainly there will be no one to see it."

"No, Vladmir, you are wrong," Edith contradicted. "Then we shall know, even as we are now known."

"That is part of a discussion I can remember having with you before." The professor paused, knocked his pipe into the ashtray and looked silently at John for a long moment.

"Professor, may I ask a question?" broke in Ken Baker. "John keeps telling us about 'the other world', the one from which this thing has displaced him. Is there any possible way he could make his way back to that other world?"

Vladmir Hilding thoughtfully ran his hand across his bald head before answering. "No, my friend. There is no way for John to go back to that 'other world' because that world does not exist; indeed, now, it has never existed. John's father, after that night and in all the subsequent actions of his life, has been obliterated by his truly untimely annihilation. He died that night and nothing can give him that earthly life again, even if Doctor Canning can give you comfort and assurance about a life to come. Nothing now can change the fact he died and did not live to do the things that now only John can remember him doing. He did not marry. He never fathered a son. He never held ten thousand conversations nor did any thing he might have otherwise done, regardless of what John now thinks he remembers. John's memories are now the stuff of dreams. They truly never happened. John is going to have to make the best of things as he now finds them. There is nothing for him to go back to, and no way he might start out."

"It seems to me you are overlooking something, Hilding" interposed Edith Canning. "Suppose you could direct NASA to dispatch a rocket to intercept that object that by your analysis is now on its approach to the earth. Could you not cause that explosion to take place harmlessly in space, destroying the object and preventing the death of John's father at the end of its interrupted trajectory?"

The physicist smiled. "Yes, at first glance, that would certainly seem to be possible. If I had the influence in Washington to get them to spend a multibillion dollar 'bird' on such a purpose, I could calculate the necessary coordinates to enable such a collision to take place. But if I did, then what would be the result? John would have the experience of finishing his sermon at Centerville and going home with his wife for Sunday Dinner. But then a paradox arises. I would never have heard of the Invisible Radiating Anomaly, would be unaware of its existence, and would therefore not have dispatched a missile to intercept it, so it would not, in fact, have been intercepted and would continue on its way to its rendezvous of death. But then, I would again have studied it and would send up the intercepting agent, in which case... ."

He drew his coffee cup across the table and stared into its tepid remains. "I don't know what would happen in the face of such temporal oscillation and what the consequences might be of such a thing on the fabric of our reality; and I do not propose we attempt to find out."

Valerie could not restrain herself any longer. "Professor, did the object, the 'CT Meteor,' enter the atmosphere near where John Masters was preaching that Sunday? Is that why it had its effect upon him at that precise moment?"

"My dear young lady, no." came the reply. "There was no direct link between your friend John and the object at any time. It was his father who was affected by it. It seems likely that about three hundred and sixty seconds after it encountered the earth's atmosphere in its time frame, it exploded on the ground in Western New York State, and from that moment the John Masters preaching in that pulpit can no longer exist. But John has himself never been any closer to that object than he is right now."

He stopped and turned his full, intense attention upon John. After a long pause, he said softly, "But there is the one great unresolved problem. There remains the one thing I cannot account for with my theory. That is you, John. If all of this is true, and I am now completely sure it is, where did you come from and what are you doing here? How can you possibly exist?"

FORTY-FOUR

♦

Across the street from the motel, two men sat in the darkness in their parked car. They had spent all evening sitting there, watching and quietly waiting for the time when the rental car would return and disgorge the party from Colorado, registered in those two adjacent motel units. From time to time they spoke with each other, but most of the hours passed in silence. Now, as they watched, the white Ford swung in from the street and pulled into its parking place. Two figures got out and then the car backed out again and drove off down the street. The dark figure sitting on the driver's side of the parked vehicle said simply, "that's them, the Masters. Baker has driven off with the other girl."

"Perfect. I'll never get a better chance," came the reply in the darkness. The speaker opened the door opened and stepped out. He walked quickly across the street and approached the doorway into which John and Jan had just disappeared. When he got to the door he paused briefly and then firmly knocked.

Jan responded to the sound. "Yes. What is it?"

"I need to speak to Reverend Masters, please. It is quite important."

It was John himself who swung the door open and stood confronting the man who stood on the step. After a moment he said, "I don't know you."

"No, Reverend, I acknowledge you don't. We have never met. But I have been looking forward to meeting you and talking with you about our situation, and about your own."

"How did you know where to find me?"

The man laughed. "It wasn't easy. We first became aware of you

211

late last month and I have been trying to get a line on you ever since. Yesterday I phoned the office at St. Matthew's in Denver and the secretary let it slip you were with Ken Baker somewhere, although as usual she was very close-mouthed about where that might be. We had gotten a Journal for the Colorado Conference when we first heard about you, and thought you were a member of that conference when we were looking for the church you were serving. It was easy for us to look up Ken Baker and to call his church. Fortunately, his secretary had not been so carefully instructed and she said you folks were here in Berkeley. After that it wasn't too hard to check the registration at the motels here in town by phone until we found you. We told them we were friends and had promised to get together but had lost the name of the motel, and they were happy to tell us you were registered here."

"You are the one who has been making the mysterious telephone calls to Jim Braddock's office," John pursued.

"Mea culpa," grinned the other. "May I come in and talk with you? I believe you might be interested in what I have to say."

John stood aside and the newcomer came into the small, well-lighted room. Jan emerged from the bathroom and the stranger nodded in greeting.

"Mrs. Masters. My name is Henry Worden and I am here to offer your husband a church. That is as sinister as things are going to get, I assure you. Not that this has not been a cloak and dagger operation, at least on my part."

He turned again to John and, following the latter's gesture, took a seat in one of the plastic motel chairs while John sat on the edge of the bed and Jan sat on the settee.

"One of my friends, the one who first heard about you and was led to believe you were the pastor God had for us, took it upon himself to steal the card for your motel registration the morning you left Lakeland. He did it on the spur of the moment and has been feeling guilty ever since, but if it had not been for that lapse in ethics we would not have known where to find you, and I guess nothing has been really harmed by his act. I am sorry if this business has been a bit mysterious but, under the circumstances, it is hard to see any other way we would have felt comfortable in contacting you until we know where you stand. But, as of tonight, if you turn out to be a completely committed 'conference man' and not at all interested in being our pastor, and so tell the superintendent what is going on, it still will not matter. The escrow closes tomorrow. I am sure it is too late now for anyone to stop the sale from going through."

John's only reply was to look puzzled and wait.

The man who called himself Henry Worden sat back and crossed his legs. "Let me start at the beginning. I have spent my life in the United Connectional Church and always have been what was accounted a 'good church member,' but I really came to understand what it was all about at a Lay Witness Mission in our church some five years ago. All these folks came so far to share with us the difference Christ was making in their lives. I looked at Christ and the church in a whole new light during those three days, and I came alive to the real possibilities for me in the Christian life. I became involved in a men's fellowship group and began to be aware of the emphasis on the Holy Spirit and His Gifts. Our pastor at the time was completely open to our ministries and experiences that followed being 'baptized with the Spirit' and our church really began to grow.

"In the course of the next two years I would guess we added two-, maybe three-hundred members, and we really came alive. Then, two years ago, our pastor moved to another church and our present minister came. He was a different sort than his predecessor had been and was most interested in building a new church and relocating out where, as he said, 'we would have room to grow and fulfill our potential.'

"Those of us—quite a large group by now—who were involved in renewal didn't see why this could not be part of God's plan, and if the pastor thought it was a good idea, well, we were willing to go along with it. So we were active in the planning and the fund-raising and all of that, going personally beyond our tithes to see that it would be completely paid for when the old building was sold. The long and the short of it is that we have a fine new building we moved into last month. Things seemed to be really great. Some of us were a bit unhappy to give up the familiar old church, but then those feelings are always there and are the price that is paid for progress.

"Then we got it between the eyes, as they say. Our pastor got up in the new church just after Easter and told us he was tired of our 'superstition' and he was not going to 'put up with' our 'fanaticism' any longer. We could 'forget this nonsense or leave,' and he didn't care which. I was shocked and hurt and I couldn't believe my ears. I went to him the next day and tried to talk him into some kind of accommodation, but he wouldn't hear of it. Our prayer groups were to stop meeting at the church at once, and they were to cease altogether regardless of where they could find to meet; else we would be excluded from all participation in any part of the church and would be dropped from the membership rolls."

John frowned. "He can't do that."

"It might not be legal according to that Discipline Book the church is supposed to go by, but I assure you he is capable of trying it, and the people I represent are not going to tear the church apart in some kind of fight. We met in my home the next evening and prayed most of the night before we decided to give him what he wanted. We would pull out with as much love as we could muster, and form our own church. We suspected, if push came to shove, the conference hierarchy would support our minister's decision against us; so we decided we would have to become a separate church, starting out with maybe a hundred and fifty members. But we figured a hundred and fifty dedicated, Spirit-filled, tithing members could swing it; and we agreed that night to try to buy our old church building that was still awaiting sale. We would keep a low profile and move to buy the old site and then, on Pentecost, we would be ready to begin functioning as a newborn faithful church. We knew the pastor would not sell to us if he knew what was cooking, so I had my attorney make the offer, representing himself as acting for a new group, The Faith Fellowship Church, wanting to locate in the community. It was accepted and, as I said, tomorrow the escrow closes and we get title and possession. So our pastor is happy to have sold the old plant (though I doubt he will be so happy when he discovers how many of his best givers he has driven away from the support of his budget) and we are really happy having our comfortable and familiar church back, with a new opportunity to serve Christ in the way we feel He is calling us to serve."

"And your pastor knows nothing about your plans?"

"Not a thing. As far as he is concerned, we have caved in and decided to submit and remain. That's the way it will be until we open our doors on Pentecost, June 3rd, three Sundays from now. All we lack is a pastor to lead us.

"Then, last month, one of our members was on a short vacation at the Lake—Skylake, of course—and he attended a meeting as a visitor when you happened to be present with Mrs. Masters. He was really impressed with you, but he also felt the Lord was telling him you would be the one for us. He found out from that lady pastor (isn't she great?) that you were United Connectional, although she didn't seem to know where you were serving. Well, he went back to his room to pray and then when he went looking for you to talk to you, you folks had left. Then, as I said, he panicked to think he would lose you and we wouldn't be able to find you; and he acted like some 'private eye' in the movies, sneaking in and stealing your registration card with your home address and all. But I guess I am glad he did. So we come down to the real question. Are you free and might you be interested in our church? Or will you blow the whistle on us?"

John grinned. "I guess there are a lot of questions I should ask first, about housing and salary and organization and the rest. One question I will ask: where is this?"

"Orchardview, near San Jose. We were—are—part of the Old St. John's United Connectional Church there."

"Yes, I know the church. Nice town, nice building. But before we go any further, you had better know I find myself in irregular circumstances. I am a seminary graduate but my seminary will not acknowledge the fact. I am a member of this annual conference but they no longer recognize me. I have just been told there is no scientific reason for me to be alive at all, even though my health is and has been excellent. I truly believe it. I am a Pastor-Teacher and have dreamt of a church like the one you are offering me, but I am now very, well— anomalous. If you attempt to investigate me you are going to come up short, empty-handed and confused."

Harry grinned and shook his head. "Tell me about it. As if we haven't already discovered that, with a vengeance. Except for the folks at St. Matthew's in Denver, we haven't found anyone who will even admit you exist or that they have ever heard of you. If it wasn't for Barry's conviction that you are the one... But I guess the one question that I have to ask is the one I heard asked once when I was an alternate member at the annual conference session: 'Is there anything against your character?'"

John laughed. "Nothing, 'Bishop.' If you were able to talk to the people whom I served in twenty years of ministry they might not feel, each and all, that I was 'the greatest pastor they ever had' but none of them would have anything of which to accuse me. I have never had to leave a church because of ministerial misconduct or scandal, and the large majority always acted as if they were reluctant to see me go. But just how do you know I am the minister you want for your church? You have never heard me preach, and you really and literally cannot know anything about me. There are lots of preachers around."

Now Harry laughed. "My words, exactly, and that has been my position throughout the discussions we have been having and why I got the job of coming here tonight. We operate in our new fellowship by consensus. A majority decision may be a decision of the flesh, and we feel God will lead us to complete accord if we make that the necessary precondition for a decision to act. If somebody still has doubts even when everyone else is for action, we wait and pray and continue to discuss the possibilities.

"Well, Barry came back from the Lake convinced God had told him you were the minister we were looking for. We prayed about it and two separate prophecies came that confirmed everything Barry had said. One by one they became convinced you were God's man for us, even in the face of the stone wall we ran into when we tried to find out about you and your past. I was put off by the mystery about you, and I guess I was upset by what Barry had done to get your address and enable us to make contact with you. Anyway, I wanted interviews and a trial sermon and maybe several candidates. But, one by one, my brothers were convinced Barry's leading was of the Lord, and they argued with me that it would be no different than it had always been for us. The bishop, the superintendent, the cabinet made a decision about who should be our new pastor, and the first time we heard him and knew what he was like was when he had come and moved into the parsonage and was in the middle of his first Sunday. Now it was God Himself doing the same thing, and if we trusted God working through the denominational structure surely we could trust Him when He worked directly and without the middle-men. Finally it was agreed that since I was the one who still did not agree, I should come and talk with you myself and see if the Lord would lead me to agree with the rest and to offer you the position."

"Well, here we are. What is the Lord saying to you now?"

Harry Worden was clearly a happy man. "We operate, as I said, by consensus. To start with, we can see our way clear to offer fifty thousand a year, a house, and utilities. And you run our church the way you would run any United Connectional Church, except with no district or conference or denominational strings. And you help us to grow in our ministries, not cut us off at the pockets. O.K.?"

John looked at his wife. "Jan, honey, what do you think?"

She smiled. "I don't think, dearest, I know."

She turned to Harry Worden. "Mr. Worden, the answer is yes. This is of God, and I know we are going to enjoy serving Christ with you."

John nodded his agreement. "You have heard it. When do we start?"

"Tomorrow if you like. I have a check here already made out with an advance of one month's salary plus an additional two thousand for moving expenses. If you and the lady will come to Orchardview tomorrow morning, we'll try to start looking for a house."

John took the check from the outstretched hand. "And you are authorized by the church to make this offer and agreement?"

"Just about the moment you opened the door, the vote became unanimous and the consensus was complete. Any other questions?"

John stepped forward and embraced Harry Worden warmly. "Thank you, Lord. I have a church again, by the grace of Christ."

"Amen," Harry answered.

As Harry returned to the waiting car, John stood in the open door watching him go, his heart dancing within him. It seemed to him that doorway now opened out onto a whole new life.

EPILOGUE

$\blacklozenge$

He took a deep breath.

Fall was unmistakably in the air in Orchardview this morning, John decided. If he had still been serving in Centerville it would not be long before the trees would be turning, burnished by rich golds and vivid reds. The trees here in this coastal valley would not be so beautiful, but there were other kinds of beauty to compensate.

Reverend John Lewis Masters, Pastor of the Faith Fellowship Church, inserted his key and opened the door to his study, thereby officially beginning another week of ministry. As he stepped into the bookshelf-lined room he first of all made himself go and change the wall calendar, moving the markers to "Tuesday" and "Eighteen" and then stood back and viewed his handiwork. Tuesday the eighteenth of September. Exactly five months since he had married Jan in this life. Five and a half months since he had awakened that morning in the debris of downtown Denver.

How confused, devastated, and forsaken he remembered feeling that morning and in the days that immediately followed. How blessed he had come to be as time passed. As it had finally turned out, he had lost nothing. His new life was better in every way than it had been before. Life here at Faith was a daily adventure of new discovery of the power and love of God in the Holy Spirit. The promise he had detected in himself after the awakening for being used by God in a ministry of healing was being wonderfully realized, day by day. His new congregation was growing both in personal grace and in numbers, week by week. And then there was Jan.

He thought back to the morning in mid-June when Jan had come to him just out of the shower, with her body still damp from the cleansing wetness, and had stood in laughing nakedness before him, visibly clothed only with joy. "Lay your hands upon me, husband, and please pray for us. We are expecting a child."

John had asked, dumbfounded, "Are you sure?"

Jan had replied, "My dearest, I am very sure. The doctor will have the opportunity this morning to confirm what I already know."

John's joy was now complete. How hard they had tried in the old life to become parents, and always without success. Now, almost as soon as they were married, Jan had conceived.

He reflected that this was only one way his marriage was better than he remembered it being. In the old life he had a good marriage with Jan, but it was far better now. He knew what the difference was, and he rejoiced in the new richness of relationship that was theirs because he knew this time how to love a wife.

He wondered if Ken Baker and his wife Valerie were also enjoying such increased joy and personal richness. They would, of course, have no way of knowing, since all of the memories and experiences of the life he had known them to have were now lost to them both. Still, when Jan had finished one of her frequent telephone sessions with Valerie, she had nothing but good things to report about the newlyweds.

The fears that had seemed so threatening in those first weeks after his awakening had now melted away. As it had been with Job in the Bible, so it was with him: *"And the Lord restored the fortunes of Job when he had prayed for his friends; and the Lord gave Job twice as much as he had before."* He had his vocation back, his wife, his dearest friends—everything that had once seemed lost. The one thing he had never lost, his faith, had also benefited from the ordeal. He now knew himself to be a far better pastor than he had ever been in those times now lost and forgotten by everyone else. He still had no seminary degree to frame and place on his wall, but in the rising tide of new non-denominational, high commitment churches like his own Faith Fellowship Church, the emphasis was upon what the pastor could do and not what academic honors he commanded. Should the time ever come when he would have to find another church to serve, he knew his spreading reputation would serve him in good stead in securing another place. Not that he was thinking about such a thing, for this church was growing daily. At the beginning of September they had added a second service on Sunday morning to accommodate everyone who wanted to attend, and it looked as if still another one would be needed, possibly as soon as the first of the year.

There was still deep sorrow when he thought about his parents. Both mom and dad had been gone for a number of years, but now they were parents who had never known the experiences of raising a child. But they had. They had been his parents, and they had done a good job of bringing him up. They had given him love, understanding, and discipline. It was hard to reconcile his memories with the scientific record that Lewis Masters had vanished into oblivion in a millionth of a second of unthinkable violence, and that his mother had married someone whom he had never known and then had died in an accident.

That brought him back to the question Professor Hilding had asked and was continuing to ask whenever they talked; the question that still remained unanswered: "Where did you come from and what are you doing here? How can you possibly exist?"

That was the unanswered question. The possibility of his being born had ended suddenly in a night-moment sixty-five years ago, and again on a San Diego street a decade later. The process by which he had come into the world had thus never been initiated nor pursued. By all of the logic of the reality that had come to be, he should simply have winked out of existence sometime during the fiery descent of that object, a moment which was so short and appeared to take so long because of the time-vector discrepancy due to its alien origin. His life had been transformed the moment it struck the atmosphere of the planet. His participation in the lives of those around him had been carefully sponged out and replaced without a trace. He was left without place or roots in a world that could do without him and had in fact done so.

Why and how, then, was he still here? He could understand the dreams that had haunted Jan's life. They had been married long enough for the mysterious fact of a God-ordained relationship to have worked to unite them into the promised "one flesh" Scripture talked about. God was honoring the "oneness" that had grown up in their marriage, and had intervened in her life through those dreams to keep her for him. Their united life was a cosmic and heavenly reality God valued and had acted to preserve and to protect in the midst of this upheaval.

But that did not answer the question. Vladmir Hilding continued to fret about the scientific explanation for his continued existence. How had he been shielded from the consequences of his father's annihilation? The physicist was insistent upon discovering the logical reason, the natural law that had somehow caused him to survive when there seemed no way for it to have happened.

"Oh Lord," John said half aloud. "if only I knew how and why it happened that I am still alive."

Look.

John heard the inner voice and looked around. His eyes settled upon the copy of the old Methodist Book of Worship lying open on his desk. Sunday, he had been preparing for a funeral that he would conduct this afternoon and had been reviewing the old and familiar form of the funeral service that utilized the King James Version in the readings from the Scriptures. Those words were of special meaning to so many people. He saw the book was still open to the page quoting from the Eighth Chapter of Romans.

Read.

John leaned over the desk and it seemed to him that several lines on the page before him grew suddenly darker and more insistent in their typography. He read:

> **"For I am persuaded that neither death nor life, nor angels nor principalities nor powers, nor things present nor things to come nor height nor depth *nor any other creature,* shall be able to separate us from the love of God that is in Christ Jesus our Lord."**

"Nor any other creature." Nor any other created thing. Only God is uncreated. And there is but one Creator. If he could accept Vladmir Hilding's idea that the piece of alien matter that had done all the damage was from another creation altogether, it was still from the hand of the One Creator. All other persons and things were the "creatures" the Apostle was referring to. Paul could, of course, know nothing of completely alien creations. But that did not diminish the power of the promise. Nothing is able to separate the Christian from the love of God.

Suddenly John saw it. Nothing—no thing, of any description— could have the power to separate those who have chosen Christ from the love of God. That promise had been impossibly fulfilled in his own experience. Out of the depths of space, from the fringes of yet another and completely foreign reality, had come that piece of debris that had

221

changed lives so completely. But it had been kept from blasting him out of existence because he had chosen Christ and trusted in Him and had thus become a child of God, an inheritor of all the promises—including this one. God Himself had intervened. He must have. That was the only possible explanation. He would not interfere with this natural event, but He could and did act to preserve His child and to keep him intact and alive against all logical possibilities. He had then carefully and gently inserted him back into reality and life in the way that would cause the least disruption in the lives and freedom of others. Where had he been on that lost Sunday afternoon and evening and all day Monday, April 2nd? He could only believe he had been in the hand of God until the morning of his awakening.

He wondered if anyone else in the world had ever known, in such a way as this, the power of the love of God and the true richness of this promise. God kept His word; and when He had taken away what had been, He had rewarded faithfulness by giving again all that had been lost, and more. It was indeed the story of Job all over again. The best church he had ever wanted, the finest wife a man could have, and now a child that had never been possible before. That would have been too much for him to lose, and so God had mercifully kept Jan from conceiving until now.

John stepped through the connecting door and into the sanctuary so that he might go before the altar to pray. All around him he felt the presence and the love of God.

This morning he could find words only for one prayer. Again and again, with increasing feeling, he repeated the words.

"Thank you, Father."

The morning sun streamed brightly through the stained glass, setting everything aglow, as if to answer faith with further promise.

The End

CPSIA information can be obtained
at www.ICGtesting.com
Printed in the USA
LVHW030354151019
634227LV00002B/308/P

9 781733 508445